| DATE DUE | | | |
|---|---|---|---|
| Mar24  77 | | | |
| Apr6  78 | | | |
| May11 78 | | | |
| May22 78 | | | |
| Apr 7  79 | | | |
| Oct26  79 | | | |
| Mar16 80 | | | |
| Feb27 81 | | | |
| Apr12  81 | | | |
| Apr30  82 | | | |
| | | | |
| | | | |

KENNETH D. MILLER, Ph.D., University of Michigan, is Professor of Physical Education at Florida State University, where he has taught since 1948, and where he has served as Head of the Department of Physical Education, Health, and Recreation and as Track Coach. He has also taught and coached at Lock Haven State College. Dr. Miller has served as President of the Southern District of the AAHPER, President of the Florida AAHPER, and Associate Editor of *JOHPER*.

BILLIE J. JONES, Ph.D., Florida State University, is Associate Professor of Physical Education at that institution. She has also taught at Oklahoma State University and Drury College. Dr. Jones has coached a number of women's teams, and was the originator and Director of the Oklahoma State Track and Field Meet for High School Girls and College Women.

# TRACK AND FIELD
# FOR
# GIRLS

**KENNETH D. MILLER**

**BILLIE J. JONES**

BOTH OF FLORIDA STATE UNIVERSITY

**SECOND EDITION**

**THE RONALD PRESS COMPANY • NEW YORK**

Library of Congress Catalog Card Number: 73–77861
PRINTED IN THE UNITED STATES OF AMERICA

# Preface

Interest in competitive athletics for girls has continued to accelerate since the publication of the earlier edition, and during this period many colleges have finally begun to indicate a long overdue awareness of the situation by offering coaching courses for women physical education majors. Assuming the rapid spread of such course-of-study innovation, a continuation of the vitally significant National Institutes for Girls' Sports and a further increase in requests for in-service training by schoolwomen who recognize their lack of competence in the teaching of high-level sports skills, the valid goal of women coaches for women's teams is finally within sight.

The purpose of the present revision is to continue to contribute toward this end through the provision of an updated and improved source of reliable information concerning track and field programs for girls. Two completely new chapters have been added—one concerned with the management and conduct of track meets; another with a consideration of suggested courses of action in response to typical problems facing the woman coach. New material has been included in each of the other chapters: historical considerations have been brought up to date, new and modified events in the hurdles and the distances have been covered in detail, and information regarding comparative performances for different skill levels has been added to the treatment of each event. Anyone interested in track and field—the coach who needs an accurate source of theoretical information, the athelete who is seeking authoritative know-how concerning strategy and tactics, the student who is looking for realistic teaching techniques, or the knowledgeable fan who simply wishes to learn more about his interest—should find this text a most useful reference.

The inclusion of the feminine point-of-view in the Second Edition, through the addition of a woman co-author who is an experienced coach in her own right, provides a plus factor which cannot help but contribute to the aim of the text in many significant ways.

KENNETH D. MILLER
BILLIE J. JONES

Tallahassee, Florida
August, 1973

# Acknowledgments

The philosophy underlying the contents of this book represents contacts with literally hundreds of men and women in physical education, recreation, and athletics. The sources of various technical details, however, can be somewhat more precisely pinpointed. First credit must go to the senior author's two college coaches, Louis "Scoop" Carlson at Marin (California) Junior College, and the legendary Colonel William "Bill" Hayward at the University of Oregon. Other coaches who have exerted strong influences on this text through their writing have been George Bresnahan and W. W. Tuttle of the University of Iowa, Dean Cromwell of the University of Southern California, and, in particular, Ken Doherty of the University of Pennsylvania. Both of the authors are, of course, deeply indebted to innumerable other coaches and athletes who have contributed to their backgrounds through writings, clinics, and personal contacts.

Of particular help as a source of historical information for this book has been the little known (on this side of the Atlantic) volume, *Women's Athletics*, by the British coach, George Pallett. Mr. Pallett's progressive world record lists and his summaries of important early meets are veritable bonanzas to any student of women's track and field—particularly of the European scene.

Miss Dorothy Kannon of Florida Technological University, and Mrs. Lisa Anderson of Maclay School, Tallahassee, did the art work. Mr. Ad Gilbert, Mr. Richard Parks, and Mr. Gilbert Lawhon, all of Florida State University, provided essential photography and know-how in connection with related problems. We are grateful to each of these colleagues for such vital assistance.

Parts of some chapters are taken from articles previously written by the senior author for the *Athletic Journal*, and other materials are from his contributions to *Physical Education Activities for College Men and Women*, published by William C. Brown Company. Permission of these publishers to re-use this material is appreciated.

Finally, we both are most grateful to the hundreds of physical education major students at Florida State Univeristy and Oklahoma State University, and to the many athletes on the women's track squads at these two institutions, who have been co-learners with us over the past several years.

## Acknowledgments

We wish to thank the following for contributing the illustrations indicated: Mr. Ad Gilbert (Figures 22, 23, 26, 29, 31 and 32); the Netherlands Embassy (Figure 4); Mr. Gil Lawhon (Figures 9, 14, 27 and 37); Mr. Mikio Odo (Figure 1); Mr. Dick Parks (Figures 7, 8, 10, 11, 12, 13, 30 and 33); and World Wide Photos, Inc. (Figures 2, 3 and 5).

K. D. M.
B. J. J.

# Contents

# TRACK AND FIELD
# FOR
# GIRLS

# 1

# Lessons from History

Track and field, by its very nature, is a highly competitive sport. It has not been thought of as a recreational or carry-over activity, and, generally speaking, until very recently it has never been considered quite proper exercise for young ladies. Widespread competition of women in this sport is a relatively recent phenomenon. Certainly until after World War I, cultural mores the world over resulted in strong disapproval of such activity except as an occasional light farce of one kind or another. Through most of the years of recorded history, customs, attitudes, and folkways imbued with ethical significance not only have kept women off the track and out of the jumping pits, but, by and large, have prevented their participation in any form of competitive sports.

In the United States, the first recognition of the values inherent in sports competition for girls and women came from physical education leaders in the eastern women's colleges and girls' schools about the turn of the present century. By 1903, a remarkably well-written coaching text [1] dealing with sports activities for women had appeared, which contained chapters covering 16 different sports, including two on track and field activities. The editor of the work, Lucille Eaton Hill, then Director of Physical Training at Wellesley spoke of the, ". . . awakening of girls to the delights of athletics, together with an aroused intelligence in the desirability of possessing a strong body for both use and ornament. . . ." [2] But this liberal point of view was modified, of course, by the culture pattern, and in the introduction to this book it is also pointed out to the young woman reader that ". . . some things she had better leave to men. Fiercely competitive athletics have their dangers . . . , and the qualities they tend to develop are not womanly." [3]

[1] Lucille Eaton Hill (ed.), *Athletics and Out-Door Sports for Women* (New York: The Macmillan Co., 1903).
[2] *Ibid.*, pp. 3–4.
[3] *Ibid.*, p. 6.

Track meets for German women are reported as early as 1904, and a women's section of the *Deutsche Sportberhorde für Leichtathletik* appeared in 1918. In 1917 the *Fédération Féminine Sportive de France,* under the leadership of Mme. Alice Milliat, was founded, and two years later this organization proposed the inclusion of women's events in the Olympic Games. The Olympic Committee did not look with favor upon this request, however, and denied the petition, thus briefly postponing the inevitable.

In Austria, the *Österreichischer Leichtathletik Verband* began to promote women's sections in men's sporting clubs in 1917, and in July of the following year the world's first national championship track meet for women was held under the auspices of the national organization.

Austria, Belgium, Czechoslovakia, France, Finland, Germany, and Holland all held national championships in 1921, and by 1922 women's "championship" track meets were being conducted in the United States, but without the control of a national supervising body. In that year the Amateur Athletic Union (AAU) assumed the responsibility for women's competition on the national level, and the first official championship meet was held in 1923.

Great Britain also formally organized women's athletics on a national basis in 1922, and the first national championships of the Women's Amateur Athletic Association were held in 1923. Between 1919 and 1925, Argentina, Denmark, Italy, Japan, Norway, Poland, and Switzerland joined the parade of nations in forming women's athletic associations.

The first international track and field competition for women was staged in March of 1921 at a rather unlikely location—the shooting grounds of the famed Casino at Monte Carlo. This historically significant meet, one of several sports contests held at that time in conjunction with an international meeting of women physical educators, found girls from five European countries participating in an 11-event program that produced the following winning marks:

| | |
|---|---|
| 60-meter dash | :08.2 |
| 250-meter run | :33.6 |
| 800-meter run | 2:30.2 |
| 63-meter hurdles | :12.0 |
| 74-meter hurdles | :12.6 |
| 300-meter relay (4 × 75 meters) | :49.6 |
| 800-meter relay | 1:46.2 |
| Broad jump | 15' 5" |
| High jump | 4' 7" |
| Javelin (800 grams) | 136' 3" |
| Shot put (two hands combined) | 53' 5¼" |

In the fall of the same year, women representing six countries—Czechoslovakia, France, Great Britain, Italy, Spain, and the United States—formed a body to regulate international track and field for women, the *Fédération Sportive Féminine Internationale.* This group, under the leadership of

France's energetic Mme. Milliat, organized and conducted the first Women's Olympic Games in Paris in August of 1922. The Great Britain team was unbeatable, but the United States showed well with Camelia Sabie winning the 100-yard hurdles and the standing broad jump, Lucille Godbold winning the two hands combined 8-pound shot put, and Nancy Voorhees tying for first in the high jump. Both the hurdles and the shot put events were won with new world record marks (:14.4, and 66 feet 4½ inches).

At the 1921 organizational meeting of the FSFI, plans were made to conduct the Women's Olympics every four years, and the second Games were held in Göteborg, Sweden, in the summer of 1926. Because of some rather peculiar opposition from the International Amateur Athletic Federation and the International Olympic Committee over the use of the term "Olympic Games" for these contests, the Göteborg event was called the Second Women's World Games. The United States was not represented at Göteborg, but ten nations participated in a spectacular festival that saw five world's records established as Great Britain again dominated the competition. The splendid team effort of the British girls was overshadowed, however, by Japan's Kinuye Hitomi (see Fig. 1), who put on one of the most amazing displays of all-around skill and superb conditioning seen before or since at an international meet. Miss Hitomi won the broad jump with a world record leap, won the standing broad jump, took second in the discus throw, third in the 100 meters, fifth in the 60 meters, and sixth in the 250 meters!

In 1926, the FSFI Congress legislated several historically important decisions, including standardization of the weight of the shot at 4 kilograms (8 pounds, 13 ounces) and of the discus at 1 kilogram (2 pounds, 3¼ ounces). Another important development during the period immediately prior to the 1928 Olympics was the staging of the first indoor championships in the United States in 1927.

Women first participated in the Olympic Games at Amsterdam in 1928 as the culmination of an involved and bitter struggle beginning with Mme. Milliat's original proposal for such competition in 1919. During this decade, women's participation in athletic events had become an increasingly accepted part of the culture of much of the civilized world, and this, coupled with the fact that in the Women's World Games the distaff side was in effect conducting a popular rival program, gradually pressured the International Amateur Athletic Federation into recognizing the existence of women as a significant force in the hitherto masculine society of international sports.

The eighth congress of the IAAF, which met at The Hague in 1926, was the legislative group which finally capitulated to the ladies. Amidst stormy controversy, the Congress voted 12 to 5 to experiment with women's events in the 1928 games. The United States was for the proposal, but Great Britain, the dominant power in women's international track and

**Fig. 1.** Japan's Kinuye Hitomi, one of the greatest all-around athletes in the history of women's track and field, competing in the 800-meter run at the 1928 Olympic Games in Amsterdam.

field, was strongly opposed to any association with programs run by and for men.

Only five Olympic events for women were approved by the IAAF—100 meters, 800 meters, high jump, discus, and 400-meter relay—and spokesmen for the women were highly critical of this curtailed program of events. Some were opposed to any participation on such terms, on the basis that acceptance of the meager recognition was beneath the dignity of women's athletics, which, after all, had already achieved comparable status with men's international events through their own World Games.

The argument over the scope of the program continued in and out of committees of both the IAAF and the FSFI for the next several years, but in December of 1926 the International Committee of the FSFI, representing the various national women's organizations holding membership in the

Federation, agreed to accept the opportunity to compete in the Amsterdam Games despite the inadequacy of the limited program.

Great Britain, holding fast to its principles, did not compete in the 1928 Games, but 21 other countries were represented by women athletes who established new world records in each event on the program. Canada outscored the United States team for the international title, with the German women a close third. The lone American first place was won by Elizabeth Robinson with a :12.2 100-meter run clocking. Kinuye Hitomi, the all-around Japanese star, became a middle distance runner for this Games and was runner-up in the 800 meters.

Despite the highly successful beginning made by women in their first Olympic Games competition, the restricted program had provided a frustrating situation that did not meet the needs or the desires of their sex, and the Third Women's World Games were held, as scheduled, in Prague in 1930. The United States did not enter a team, and Germany won easily, more than doubling the score of the runner-up, Poland. Stanislawa Walasiewicz (later, in the United States, Stella Walsh), who won gold medals for Poland at three sprinting distances—60 meters, 100 meters, and 200 meters—was the outstanding performer of the Games. Miss Walasiewicz (see Fig. 2) achieved subsequent worldwide recognition as being one of the world's notable women athletes. At one period she held 30 women's records! It is of considerable interest that Miss Walsh established a new United States record score in winning the national pentathlon champion-

**Fig. 2.** Stella Walsh (Poland's Stanislawa Walasiewicz), 1932 Olympic champion at 100 meters, shown winning the AAU 200 meters championship in 1942.

**Fig. 3.** Mildred "Babe" Didrikson, second from right, winning the 80-meter hurdles final at the 1932 Olympic Games in Los Angeles. Teammate Evelyne Hall, right, was runner-up in the event.

ship in 1951 at the age of forty. Twelve years later she was still competing enthusiastically and well as an official entry in the discus throw at the 1963 National AAU Women's Championships.

At Prague, the amazing Japanese, Hitomi, won her specialty, the broad jump, and placed third in the 60-meter dash and in the javelin throw.

The 1932 Olympics were held at Los Angeles and, once again, the winning effort in each event was a new world record. Athletes representing the United States were victorious in every event except the 100-meter dash, which was won by Poland's great sprinter, Walasiewicz. The outstanding performer of the Los Angeles Games, however, was the fabulous Mildred "Babe" Didrikson, who took gold medals in the javelin throw and the 80-meter hurdles, and the second-place award in the high jump (see Fig. 3).

The versatile Miss Didrikson was several times an All-American basketball player, and a good enough pitcher to play on a men's professional baseball team. After her track heyday she achieved further athletic honors as the British Amateur golf champion, the United States Amateur golf champion, and the United States Open golf champion. She had official tournament bowling scores as high as 270, and was recognized by tennis experts as being the equal of the top amateur players in the nation (she gave up a planned tennis career when declared ineligible—the United States Lawn Tennis Association considered her a professional—before she had played in her first tournament). In 1950 "Babe" Didrikson was selected by United Press as the top female athlete of the first half of the twentieth century.

Other American first places at Los Angeles were won by Jean Shiley in the high jump, Lillian Copeland in the discus throw, and the 400-meter relay team of Mary Carew, Annette Rogers, Evelyn Furtsch, and Wilhelmina Von Bremen.

In the meanwhile, the controversy over the program for women continued unabated. At the 1932 meeting of the IAAF Congress, representatives of the Women's Federation stated a position to the effect that if a complete program were not included in subsequent Olympic Games, it would be more acceptable to have no women's events at all. Two years later, Germany proposed that the IAAF should be the sole governing body representing women's track and field. The untiring Mme. Milliat, speaking for the FSFI, left the door open for such an abdication of authority by her group, but only on the basis that a complete list of events be included in the Olympics. A joint committee of the two Federations was established to seek a mutually satisfactory solution to the problems.

The Fourth Women's World Games were conducted in London in 1934, with the German team in complete command. Nine of the 12 events were won by Germans. American women again did not compete in track and field in these Games (the United States was represented, however, by a basketball team).

Women athletes from 20 nations entered the Olympic Games held in Berlin in 1936, and world standards were expanding at such a rapid pace that even in their own backyard, the Germans failed to dominate the field as might have been expected from the results of the London World Games held just two years previously. The same six events that had been included at Los Angeles were on the program at Berlin, and new world records were established by the United States' Helen Stephens with :11.5 in the 100 meters, and by the German 400-meter relay team.

Following the Berlin Games, the IAAF Congress adopted proposals satisfactory to the women's group, and this circumstance culminated the persistent, effective efforts of the FSFI and Mme. Milliat to achieve world recognition of the right of women for equality in athletics parallel to that of their brothers.

Strangely enough, during the early war years, women's track and field performances continued to improve, and with increasing frequency the name of Holland's Francina "Fanny" Koen (later Blankers-Koen) was in the sporting news. During 1942 and 1943, in occupied Holland, she equaled the world mark for the 80-meter hurdles, and established new records in the high jump and broad jump.

During the final years of World War II, little opportunity was provided for athletic competition except in the various military services. By 1946, however, national and international events were in full swing, and the

**Fig. 4.** Netherland's Francina Blankers-Koen, the all-time greatest woman performer in track and field, shown winning one of her four gold medals at the 1948 London Olympic Games.

most obvious change in the old pattern was the full-scale emergence of the Russians as world-class performers. In the Oslo European Games, held in August of 1946, Russian women won five first places in the nine-event program.

The 1948 Olympic Games were held at London with nine events being contested by athletes from 27 countries. Blankers-Koen (see Fig. 4), the Dutch housewife, dominated the running events by winning four gold medals—100 meters, 200 meters, 80 meters hurdles, and 400-meter relay. The United States' Alice Coachman was the lone American victor, establishing a new Olympic high jump record at 5 feet 6⅛ inches.

Neither the Russians nor the Germans competed in the London Olympics. Of general interest is the fact that in a Warsaw meet in late 1948, Russian women exceeded the Olympic Games winning performances in the shot put, the discus throw, and the javelin throw. In this latter meet, both the shot and discus marks were new world records.

Also in post-Olympics 1948, Blankers-Koen performed the astonishing feat of winning five events in the Netherlands national championships—100 meters, 200 meters, 80-meter hurdles, high jump, and broad jump! By 1950 Mrs. Blankers-Koen, a mother of two children, was officially credited with the world record in each of these events except the 200 meters (which was still held by Stella Walsh), but this latter discrepancy was repudiated by her accepted world record in the 220-yard sprint. Despite the athletic brilliance of such other stellar performers as Kinuye Hitomi, Stella Walsh, and the greatest all-around athlete of all times, "Babe" Didrikson, "Fanny" Blankers-Koen stands alone as the top woman performer in the history of track and field up to the present day.

In the two decades between the Los Angeles Games and 1952, American women of world-class in track and field were conspicuous by their absence. Helen Stephens in 1936 and Alice Coachman in 1948 were our only international winners in individual events during this 20-year period. Our 400-meter relay team had won a dissatisfying first place in Berlin on a baton passing mishap by the German team, and aside from this somewhat hollow victory only Annette Rogers, Audrey Patterson, and Dorothy Dodson had been able to place in Olympic competition. Miss Rogers was the most versatile of this small band, placing in the 100 meters, the high jump, and running a leg on the winning 400-meter relay team in the 1936 Games.

Interest in track and field for women was at a low ebb in the United States during this period, and except for a few faint, frustrated voices raised in protest from women members of the AAU, there was no attempt to provide an organized program of competitive track and field for girls which would develop interest on the part of talented youngsters in schools, or would help in the search for athletes skilled enough to represent the United States adequately in international competition.

The First Pan-American Games were held at Buenos Aires in 1951. Women from the United States placed in every event except the broad jump, but Jean Patton's :25.3 200-meter time provided our only first place even though winning marks were subpar in terms of world-class performance.

Helsinki, Finland, was the scene of the 1952 Olympics, and amid a barrage of outstanding performances, American girls won the 400-meter relay in the world record time of :45.9. Mae Faggs (who also took sixth in the 100-meters—the only other American place), Barbara Jones, Janet Moreau, and Catherine Hardy made up this team that achieved the first American world record performance since Helen Stephens' victory at Berlin 16 years previously.

The most apparent lesson of the Helsinki Games was the fact that the Russians took their athletics very seriously, indeed. In the throwing events, Russian women took first, second, and third in the discus; second, third, and fourth in the javelin; and first, third, and fourth in the shot put! This formidable team power was backed up by second places in the broad jump and 80-meter hurdles, third places in the high jump and 200 meters, and fourth place in the 400-meter relay.

The obvious all-out national promotion represented in this team strength made it seem almost unkind to send our girls to the Games, and despite the success of our record-setting relay team, both the National Committee Chairman, Evelyne Hall, and the team manager-coach, Lucile Wilson, suggested that unless more support and interest were to be provided in the future, women's events should be eliminated from the United States Olympic program!

Through the next few years, European women made a shambles of the record book. Soviet girls, in particular, were dominating the world lists of best performances in all events. In 1953 alone, Russian women were responsible for six new world records, and by the end of that year the United States, for the first time since 1932, was unlisted in the 20 world records recognized by the IAAF.

The Second Pan-American Games were held in Mexico City in 1955, with a seven-event program for women. Four events were won by the United States team, and in each of these except the relay, marks were on a par with European performances of the 1955 season! Barbara Jones won the 100 meters in :11.5, Mildred McDaniel took first place in the high jump with 5 feet 6$\frac{5}{16}$ inches, and Karen Anderson won the javelin throw with 161 feet 3 inches.

These performances at Mexico City provided a badly needed lift. After Helsinki, women's track in this country—ignored by school physical educators, national athletic officials, developmental committees, and the public at large—had reached a new low in esteem, and the morale of the few girls and women struggling to keep the sport alive had been in a state of decline.

Largely through the efforts of a very effective National Committee, ably chaired by Mrs. Roxanne Anderson, conditions had improved steadily since 1952, and the United States girls surprised the world at the Melbourne Olympic Games four years later by ranking third behind the U.S.S.R. and Australia in the unofficial team standings. Our top performer was Mildred McDaniel, who demonstrated that her Pan-American victory was only a start, by establishing a new Olympic and world record in winning the high jump gold medal with 5 feet 9¼ inches. Other American girls placed in the 100 meters, broad jump, discus throw, shot put, and 400-meter relay. One of the United States relay team members was a 16-year-old named Wilma Rudolph of whom more was to be heard later.

Less startling to the world of women's sports than the quality of the United States team, but still largely unexpected, was the strength of Australia in winning four gold medals to Russia's two. Betty Cuthbert won the 100 meters and the 200 meters, equaling the Olympic record of :11.5 in the 100, and equaling both the world and Olympic records of

:23.4 in the 200. Shirley Strickland de la Hunty established a new world and Olympic mark of :10.7 in winning the 80-meter hurdles, and the Australian girls' 400-meter relay team posted a new world and Olympic record of :44.5 in winning that event.

The Third Pan-American Games were held in Chicago in 1959 after a succession of other cities in North, Central, and South America were forced to withdraw their bids for the privilege of staging the festival. The United States team responded to the location and to an excellent pregames developmental program by winning eight of the ten events.

None of the winning marks at Chicago was attention-getting in terms of world-class performance, but a significant lesson was pointed out in the fact that six of the United States' eight championships were won by co-eds from Tennessee State University, one of the few schools in this country at that time which sponsored a women's track and field team and provided high-level coaching of the quality found with similar programs for men.

The year prior to the 1960 Olympiad saw a flurry of international world-class performances. Russia's Maria Itkina posted :53.4 for 400 meters and and :53.7 for 440 yards, both world records, and Betty Cuthbert set new world standards of :07.2 in the 60-meter dash, and :23.2 in the 220-yard dash. Germany's Gisela Birkemeyer clocked a :10.5 80-meter hurdles, and the Russians Elvira Ozolina and Tamara Press established records in the javelin throw (195 feet 4½ inches) and shot put (58 feet 4 inches) which seemed unbeatable except by themselves.

Of particular interest to Americans was the :22.9 mark for 200 meters posted by the United States' Wilma Rudolph prior to the Olympic team trials. Up to this point, Miss Rudolph had been just another good sprinter from Tennessee State; subsequently she was the world's best.

The 1960 Olympic Games were held in Rome, and Russia's nationalistic approach to this international competition paid off handsomely as the U.S.S.R. women improved on their Melbourne record by taking six gold medals, and placing finalists in every event on the program—a program, incidentally, in which new Olympic records were set in each event. In two contests the amazing Russians had three places in the first six, and in four other events they had two of the top six places. It was only the continuance of Germany's emergence as the second world power in women's track and field that made the Games much of a contest. Although the Germans did not win a single gold medal, they placed in seven events, and had multiple finalists in three.

One of the stars of the Games was the United States' Rudolph (see Fig. 5), who proved herself to be the fastest woman runner in history by establishing new Olympic records in winning the 100 meters, the 200 meters, and anchoring the 400-meter relay team. Miss Rudolph's winning time in the 100 was a fabulous :11.0 (unfortunately, wind conditions were in excess of the permissible maximum for a world record).

The American relay team (once again, the Tennessee State University

**Fig. 5.** Wilma Rudolph shown winning the 200 meters final at the 1960 Olympic Games in Rome.

girls' varsity team) of Martha Hudson, Barbara Jones, Lucinda Williams, and Wilma Rudolph, established a new world record of :44.4 in winning their semifinal heat.

The dependable Earlene Brown was the only other United States woman to place at Rome, taking third in the shot put and sixth in the discus throw.

Following the Rome Olympics, new records were established so frequently as to become almost commonplace. An unheralded North Korean, Shin Keum Dan, started the parade by posting world marks of :53.0 for 400 meters and 2:01.2 in the 800. Over the span of the next four years, Shin had lowered her 400 mark to :51.2, and had surpassed the two-minute barrier in the 800 on three occasions. Her best 800 meters time was a 1:58 flat clocking made at Pyongyang during the summer of 1964. Rumania's Olympic champion, Iolanda Balas, erased another long-standing psychological barrier by setting a fantastic 6-foot 3¼-inch record in the high jump, and the Soviet Union's Tamara Press pushed her own shot put standard to 60 feet 10¾ inches and approached the 200-foot goal with the discus. Another of the great Russian champions, Elvira Ozolina, constantly threatened the 200-foot mark in the javelin throw, finally hitting 201 feet 4½ inches during the summer preceding the Tokyo Games. Australia's Dixie Willis and Betty Cuthbert, Russia's Tatyana Schelkanova, and the United States' fine sprinters—Wilma Rudolph, Willye White, Ernestine Pollards, and Vivian Brown—all established new records during the exciting period between Rome and Tokyo.

The Fourth Pan-American Games were held in São Paulo in May of 1963, and the most interesting outcome was the performances of two teenage schoolgirls, Canada's Nancy McCredie, who won gold medals in both the shot put and discus throw, and the United States' Eleanor Montgomery, who won the high jump.

In a long-overdue developmental program providing a series of international meets, a United States team toured Europe during the summer of 1963, and gained invaluable experience in their meets with the Russians, the Poles, the Germans, and the British national women's teams. The U.S.S.R. ground out a methodical and relentless victory over our outclassed girls, allowing the United States only the solace of two second places with which to break the monotony of the uncontested third and fourth spots in the ten-event program. Against the other, less formidable teams, however, the Americans did well. Wins were even posted in such events as the javelin throw and the 800-meter run—unheard of happenings!

Tokyo hosted the Eighteenth Olympiad in the fall of 1964, and again, as at Rome, the record book was rewritten as Olympic or world marks were set or equalled in each of the eleven events. The Russians, although winning only two first places, dominated the women's competition. Medals were well scattered among the eight leading national teams, but the U.S.S.R. women showed awesome team strength in placing athletes in the top six of every event except the 100 meters, with three finalists in both the shot put and the javelin. Germany was almost as impressive with entrants qualifying for the finals in seven events.

As usual, the Americans were in complete control of the sprints, and were out of their league in the other contests. Wyomia Tyus and teammate Edith McGuire won the 100 and 200, respectively, and the U.S. relay team of Willye White, Tyus, Marilyn White, and McGuire won the silver medal (with a time which bettered both the former world and Olympic records!) in that event.

Winnipeg was the site of the 1967 Fifth Pan-American Games, and although the United States won eight titles, only Madeline Manning's 2:02.3 800 meters (with Doris Brown a good second in 2:02.9), and Eleanor Montgomery's defense of her São Paulo high jump victory, with a world-class 5 feet 10 inches, were encouraging wins.

During this period, European women were busily negating "ultimate" performances. Liesel Westermann, of West Germany, demonstrated that 200 feet was just another measurement when she threw the discus 200 feet 11¾ inches in the fall of 1967, and in the following year she also became the first woman to surpass the 205-foot mark. East Germany's Margitta Gummel and the Soviet's Nadyezhda Chizhova were two others who drew attention during the months prior to Mexico City, with shot put distances in excess of 60 feet.

The Nineteenth Olympiad was held in the rarefied atmosphere of Mexico

City in the fall of 1968, but the shortage of oxygen seemed to have little ill effect on the women athletes of the world as they repeatedly shattered world and Olympic records in trials and finals.

Of particular joy to long-suffering American track supporters was the almost incredible fact that the U.S. team qualified entrants for the final rounds in seven events! These finalists, solidly backed by three gold medal performances, established our team unofficially as the world's best—a situation which hadn't even been dreamed of for almost four decades! The American golds were won by Tyus who repeated her 1964 win in the 100 meters with a new Olympic record of :11.0; our world record-setting relay team composed of Barbara Ferrell, Margaret Bailes, Mildrette Netter, and Tyus; and Madeline Manning who refused to be awed by the pre-Games favorites, and simply ran away from the field in the 800 meters, clocking a new record of 2:00.9 in the process.

The Russians, although also placing finalists in seven events, were not as intimidating as they had been at Tokyo and Rome. For the first time since the Soviet Union entered the Olympic competition at Helsinki in 1952, not a single Russian won a championship. Other Eastern European countries took up the slack in the field events, however, effectively monopolizing these contests. East Germany, Hungary, Rumania, and Czechoslovakia divided the gold awards, with Rumanian girls winning both the discus and the long jump.

The summer of 1969 started as though the team championship claimed by our girls at Mexico City was the beginning of a new day for American track and field. In July the U.S. team shocked the world by defeating the Russians (who had a previous win over the strong East Germans) at Los Angeles, for the first time ever, and it seemed as though 1932 was here again. In August, however, it was "back to the drawing board," as the touring Americans lost in Europe to West Germany and to Great Britain with generally mediocre efforts in both meets.

Other aspects were normal in European track circles that summer, too. Russia's Chizhova pushed the shot 67 feet 1/4 inch; Jaroslava Jehlickova, of Czechoslovakia, ran 1500 meters in 4:10.7; West Germany's Westermann hit 209 feet 10 inches with the discus; and France's Nicole Duclos and Colette Besson both clocked :51.7 in the 400 meters.

One additional thing was quite evident during that fantastic summer: the Germans were coming, the Germans were coming!

The year 1970 belonged to Chi Cheng. During this period, this remarkable athlete posted world records at 100 yards, 100 meters, 220 yards, 200 meters, and in the 100-meter hurdles! Jamaica's Marilyn Neufville, with a :51.0 400 meters, and West Germany's Heidi Rosendahl, with a 22 feet 5 1/4 inches long jump also established new world marks in 1970.

Cali, Colombia, was the location of the Sixth Pan-American Games in 1971. Five gold medals were won by the United States' team, but the over-all results were disappointing in that Canada and Cuba both outscored the U.S. women in unofficial team points. Aside from Iris Davis' :11.2 victory in the 100 meters, our girls' performances did not encourage any optimism for the immediate future. Athletes from other Western Hemisphere countries who won with world-class marks included Debbie Brill, Canada's sensational high jumper, who cleared 6 feet 1/4 inch; Cuba's Carmen Romero who threw the discus 187 feet; and Jamaica's Neufville who ran :52.3 in the 400 meters.

In Europe, startling performances were the order of the day as the Munich Olympics drew closer. The two-minute barrier for 800 meters was finally cracked by West Germany's Hildegard Janze-Falck in winning her national championship in 1:58.2 (Shin Keum Dan's 1964 mark of 1:58.0 had never been accepted). Nadyezhda Chizhova of the Soviet Union pushed her shot put record to 67 feet 8 1/4 inches, and her teammate Faina Myelnik reached 212 feet 10 inches in the discus throw. West Germany's Ellen Tittel ran the mile in 4:35.4, and East German runners Karin Burneleit and Karin Balzer turned in new records of 4:09.6 in the 1500 meters and :12.6 in the 100-meter hurdles, respectively. Most shocking of all, perhaps, was the fact that Balas' 1961 "incredible" 6-foot 3 1/4-inch high jump was finally bettered. Austria's Ilona Gusenbauer erased this long-standing mark by clearing 6 feet 3 1/2 inches for a new world record.

Marked by tragedy, dissension, and confusion, the Twentieth Olympiad was held in Munich during the summer of 1972. As they had been promising to do through their performances subsequent to the Mexico Games, the Germans ran roughshod over the women of the rest of the world. Together, the East German and West German teams won ten of the 14 track and field contests! East Germany had medal winners in every event except the long jump, high jump, and discus—six gold, four silver, and three bronze. The West Germans were close behind in the scoring with four wins, two seconds, and a third.

The Russians won three championships, each with a world record performance: Chizhova in the shot put, Myelnik in the discus throw, and Lyudmila Bragina in the 1500 meters. The Soviet's pre-Mexico City depth, though, was still missing. Nijole Sabaite with a silver in the 800 meters was their only other medal winner.

The Americans? Aside from very good performances from our quarter-milers and a noteworthy 196-foot 8-inch bronze medal javelin throw by Kathy Schmidt, our girls did about as expected—we were out of our league. Kathy Hammond took third in the 400 meters with a sparkling :51.7, and teamed with Mabel Ferguson, Madeline Manning, and Cheryl Toussaint to anchor the U.S. 1600-meter relay team to a pleasantly surprising second place finish. In the Americans' traditionally strong events, the sprints, we ran fourth in the 100 meters and in the 400-meter relay, and failed to qualify for the 200 finals.

The decade prior to the Munich Games was a most remarkable one in terms of the progress made in women's track and field throughout the world. The American program generally shared in this steady improvement, but not proportionately, and except in a few isolated instances, ground was lost. It was evident that a much greater effort would be necessary to close the gap between the performances of our women and those of the European nations. It was just as apparent that the major focus of any such attempt would have to be directed toward the development of an extensive national pool of talent among our youngsters. Leaders in American swimming had demonstrated the effectiveness of such a program, and had clearly indicated the guidelines for getting the job done. In the meantime, there were a few positive signs to the effect that tomorrow would be a brighter day: the increased interest in track and field for girls among school women during the early 1970s; the ever-growing rapport between leaders of the AAU and the DGWS; the rapid growth of collegiate competition; and the spreading addition of track skill development and coaching theory courses to physical education teacher training curricula, were all trends in the right direction—trends hopefully leading toward the realization of the estimable goal of represenative performances by our women in international competition.

# 2

# Getting in Shape

## BACKGROUND

Before a girl is able to perform competitively in athletics on any adequate level, she must prepare herself through two closely related processes. First, she must develop skill in the performance of the particular events in which she plans to compete, and, second, she must condition herself physically and mentally for the total effort involved in such competition. Obviously, these two—the development of skill, and the development of the degree of fitness needed to perform that skill well—normally are concomitant procedures in the training of any athlete. Despite their interdependence, however, these concepts represent separate aims, and the latter objective, the so-called "conditioning" of the girl athlete, is the primary concern of this chapter.

Conditioning refers to the gradual increase of physical and psychological readiness through a training program regulating as closely as possible the exercise, the diet, and the periods of rest and relaxation experienced by the athlete. These factors cannot be controlled precisely under normal living conditions, of course, but the attempt of the coach is to establish prescribed habit patterns of behavior which will contribute as effectively as possible toward the improvement of the girl's fitness. Both the physical and the psychological aspects of the conditioning process have hereditary limits, but within these restrictions, the closer together one can push the physiological limit (the breaking point) to the psychological limit, the greater will be the resulting performance.

An essential first step in any sound conditioning program is a thorough medical examination by a physician. Such an examination should be given to each girl athlete annually, preferably just prior to the beginning of the fall preseason training period.

## OFF-SEASON TRAINING

Training for a serious track and field effort should be a long-range, year-around operation, but the conditioning process should not be devoted

19

entirely to track and field activities throughout the year. After the competitive season is over, it is highly desirable for the girl or woman athlete to continue regular but less intensive participation in some vigorous sport other than track. A shift of interest to swimming, tennis, or *any* other demanding physical activity will prove invaluable in bringing the girl to the beginning of the preseason training period in good shape physically and, of more importance, mentally refreshed by the variation in activity for the beginning of the rigorous track program ahead. Two or three good workouts each week will do an entirely adequate job of maintaining a satisfactory level of condition throughout the late summer and early fall.

## PRESEASON TRAINING

For the best welfare of the athlete, conditioning should not be conducted as a crash program. Despite the prevalence of such procedures in most American school athletic programs, the physiological aspects of the concept of a gradual approach to condition are well known to research workers, to medical practitioners, and, obviously enough, to foreign coaches and athletes. Sound conditioning is not a short-term process, and the preseason program should extend over a period of about eight months.

Preseason work should consist primarily of activities designed to increase strength and endurance. These factors are the basic physical elements of fitness implied in the term *condition*.

### STRENGTH

Strength, because of its importance in the concept of power, is the single most important factor in athletic performance. Strength is also a physical characteristic that can be increased by simple, clear-cut procedures *if* a person has the desire to do so. Without motivation, strength is not at all easy to build simply because the only way to achieve this end is through hard work. Since additional strength will improve any athlete's performance, however, and since the typical athlete is highly motivated toward this goal, it may be stated that strength is relatively easy to increase.

Muscles become stronger when a work load greater than any previous work load is applied to the muscular effort. This is the overload principle, and should be understood by the girl athlete as well as by her coach. Frequency of repetitions of a muscular effort, without overloading, has no effect on the increase of strength.

As a muscle increases in strength, the size of the individual muscle fibers grows, resulting in an increase in muscle girth. This cross-sectional increase is due to an enlargement of existing muscle fibers, an increase in the amount of connective tissue in the muscle, and an increase in the number of capillaries.

## ENDURANCE

Endurance is the second physical trait that receives major emphasis during the fall training program. Endurance is the ability of a muscle to prolong activity without fatigue, and since this also is a basic characteristic of successful athletic performance, the athlete is normally as highly motivated toward increasing this factor as she is with increasing strength.

Like strength, the development of endurance is relatively simple and straight-forward provided the girl has the desire to achieve this end. Endurance is increased when sustained loads are placed on the muscles for increasing periods of time. The emphasis in developing endurance is on the number of contractions of a muscle rather than the resistance to which the muscle is subjected.

The physiological change that accompanies an increase in endurance is an increased capillarization within the muscles, permitting a greater fuel supply and a more efficient removal of waste products.

## CONDITIONING ACTIVITIES

The development of both strength and endurance requires perseverance of a high order, and this is a virtue which often breaks down under the weight of sheer boredom. In order to minimize this effect, the preseason program should include a variety of exercises selected from such physical conditioning activities as *fartlek,* interval training, weight training, and circuit training.

*Fartlek.*  This type of training is an ideal general conditioning activity, and is highly recommended for building endurance through the fall and winter months. The term *fartlek* is a Swedish word that can be translated roughly as "speed play." *Fartlek* consists of running (preferably cross-country or on a golf links, but many athletes use this concept around the perimeter of a football field or even on a standard track) at an easy pace interspersed, at the athlete's will, by all-out sprints and fast middle distance runs. The freedom of the runner's choice in speed variation is the factor that takes the pressure off the athlete and keeps the training routine "play" to a degree which it could never be directly under the watchful eye of a coach.

Actually, of course, to prove effective as a method of developing endurance, *fartlek* must be physically demanding. The sprinting and middle distance striding that alternate with the recovery jogging must consist of hard, purposeful efforts. There is no easy road to building endurance no matter what name is given to the process.

Novice runners will have to be oriented to rigorous training, and it is recommended that *fartlek* be the only endurance running activity for the first three or four weeks of the fall training period. During this time, the coach should discuss the day's work plan with each girl daily, and should evaluate the workout of each athlete at the end of every practice session. These first few weeks of training are important psychologically as well as physiologically, and a program in which the girl and her coach can get to know each other through the mutual planning of a training exercise which is never forced can provide the basis for a most effective pupil-teacher relationship—the foundation of successful coaching.

**Interval Training.**    This is an endurance building program in which a specific running distance is repeated a specific number of times at a specific pace.    These three factors are tied together with a specific recovery period of jogging between the repetitions.    Under the recommended gradual conditioning program, the athlete should begin interval training in the fall, after three to four weeks of *fartlek,* at a slow pace, and increase the pace each four weeks throughout the preseason training period.

One of the major advantages of this exercise is its flexibility.    Any of the factors can be modified to meet individual needs, unusual conditions, or even idiosyncrasies that may be psychologically important to an athlete.

A suggested distance for girls' interval training is 300 yards starting with three repetitions at a 60-second pace.    As the athlete's endurance improves, the pace and/or the number of repetitions can be increased.    In selecting a beginning recovery period time between repetitions, it is advisable to rely on the way the runner feels.    It is important that the girl be fresh enough to maintain the pre-established pace, and both breathing and heart-rate should be near normal before an additional repetition is attempted.

**Weight Training.**    Weight training is a program of exercises that can contribute to the general fitness, the attractive appearance, and the physical ability of girls and women by increasing strength, endurance, flexibility, and power.    This is a program in which an initial number of repetitions of prescribed exercises is gradually increased until a preset maximum number has been reached, at which time additional resistance is added to the exercise and the number of repetitions reverts to the starting figure.

Weight training is still often confused with weight lifting simply because both activities employ similar equipment.    Weight lifting, however, is a distinct sport in itself; it is a competitive activity in which the goal is to lift more poundage than an opponent is able to raise.    Weight training, on the other hand, is a program aimed at improving general fitness or performance ability in some particular sport.

Weight training is advantageous for the performer in any track and field event, and it is an essential phase of the conditioning program for

**Fig. 6.**    Suggested weight training exercises for women.

| | |
|---|---|
| 1  Military Press. | 7.  Heel Raise. |
| 2.  Two-Arm Curl. | 8.  Abdominal Curl. |
| 3.  Standing Forward Arm Raise. | 9.  Supine Pullover. |
| 4.  Rowing Exercise. | 10.  Prone Lateral Arm Raise. |
| 5.  Upright Rowing Exercise. | 11.  Supine Lateral Arm Raise. |
| 6.  Half Squat. | 12.  Supine Bench Press. |

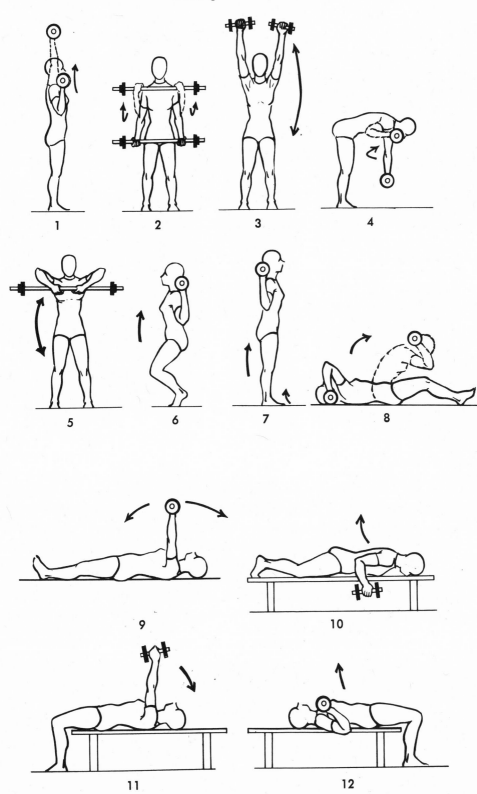

1

2

3

4

5

6

7

8

9

10

11

12

the shot putter, the discus thrower, and the javelin thrower. This is a way to strength, and strength is basic to the power complex needed for successful performance in the weight events.

During the off-season, weight training should be practiced one or two days each week, alternating with whatever sport activity the girl is participating in as a variation from her track and field event. In the fall and winter, the girl athlete should work out with the weights two or three days each week.

The beginning weight for any exercise is selected by determining the load that the girl can handle in good form for eight continuous repetitions (one set) of the exercise in question. Each repetition should be fast and powerful, but some difficulty should be experienced with the eighth repetition. After each two subsequent exercise periods, the girl should add one repetition until she reaches a set of 12. At this point 5 pounds are added to the bar, or 2½ pounds to each dumbbell, and a new series is begun with eight repetitions.

Suggested exercises are illustrated in Fig. 6. It is recommended that the beginner start her weight-training program by using the six odd-numbered exercises on one day and alternating with the six even-numbered exercises on the subsequent day of weight training.

**Circuit Training.** This is a method of conducting a conditioning program in which the athlete moves as rapidly as she can from one station to another, performing a specific resistance exercise or other conditioning activity at each stop. Typical stations may include some calisthenic exercise such as 15 push-ups, a specific weight-training set, or a rope-skipping routine.

An initial time trial establishes a base criterion, and as the program progresses, the girl attempts to lower her original time for the circuit to a predetermined goal. When this standard is reached, the exercise is increased by adding repetitions at the various stations, by adding laps to the circuit, or by establishing a new time goal.

## NUTRITION

Adequate nutrition is a situation in which the body is provided with the nourishment essential to perform the demands made upon it. Since participation in competitive athletics makes extraordinary demands upon the body, the nutrition of the athlete is a vital factor in her training and conditioning program. Food taken into the body is the sole source of *fuel* for energy, *building materials* for the repair and formation of tissues, and *regulators* for the control of body functions.

### FOODS

Foods that make up the adequate diet are composed of chemical substances that are classified into three major categories—carbohydrates, fats, and proteins—plus mineral salts, water, and vitamins.

*Carbohydrates* are found in the sugars and starches of various foods. Sweets, potatoes, breads and cereals, fruits, and milk products are rich in carbohydrates. These compounds are stored in the liver and in muscle tissue in the form of glycogen, which provides the main source of fuel for muscular energy in the anaerobic stage of exertion.[1]

Fatty meats, vegetable oils, and dairy products contain an abundance of *fats*. Compounds making up these substances are known as lipids, and are stored in muscle tissue and in various deposits around the body. Fats are the primary source of fuel during mild (aerobic) exercise. Van Itallie has pointed out that almost all normal energy comes from fats.[2]

Foods rich in *proteins* are milk, eggs, meats, fish, nuts, whole grain cereals, beans, and milk products. Food proteins are made up of amino acids, which are needed in the growth of new tissue and the maintenance and repair of old. Proteins are not important as a source of food for muscle energy.[3]

*Minerals* are important agents in the development of sound bones and teeth, and they act as regulators of such various essential body processes as peristalsis, heartbeat rhythm, acid-base balance, and thyroid functioning. Obviously, inorganic salts are of vital importance to the well-being of the individual. Fortunately, these substances are present in the common foods —milk and milk products, green vegetables, lean meat, and other proteins— and assuming a balanced diet is followed, no supplementary source of these critical substances is needed in the athlete's diet.

*Water* is a primary necessity of life. This commonplace substance serves as an indispensable solvent and diluting agent, aids in the transporting of body fuels and waste products, and provides an imperative function in regulating body temperature. A water balance must be maintained; water intake must equal water loss. Most body water comes from the normal diet—from liquids and from fluids making up the "solid" foods. During exercise, or under conditions of unusual heat, small amounts of water should be taken by the athlete at frequent intervals to avoid dehydration.

Proper and adequate nutrition requires certain organic compounds called *vitamins*. These substances are essential in the maintenance of good health, and a varied, well-balanced diet will supply all the vitamin needs.

## TRAINING

### DIET

In order to assure proper nutrition, it is necessary for the athlete to follow a diet that provides a variety of nutritious foods in amounts adequate

[1] From an interview with Theodore Van Itallie, "If Only We Knew," *Nutrition Today*, 3 (June, 1968), p. 5.

[2] *Ibid.*

[3] Per-Olof Åstrand, "Something Old and Something New . . . Very New," *Nutrition Today*, 3 (June, 1968), p. 9.

to maintain her weight at an optimum level. Generally speaking, the best diet is one which she enjoys, and that is balanced in terms of including food products from each of the six categories previously considered: carbohydrates, fats, proteins, mineral salts, water, and vitamins. A balanced diet is particularly important in the provision of an adequate supply of minerals and vitamins.

Among the dietary practices recommended by nutritionists for athletes in training are the following:

1. Provide many fruits and vegetables in the diet. In addition to the value in these foods, the indigestible cellulose provides roughage, which aids elimination.
2. Schedule a regular time pattern for meals and maintain this program. Digestion proceeds most efficiently when it takes place at regular intervals.
3. Avoid fried foods, unripe or overripe fruits, freshly cooked breads, heavy gravies, and iced drinks. Such foods are difficult to digest.
4. Include milk as an item in each meal, except during the two days prior to competition, but do not use it (or any other liquid) to wash food down.
5. Serve meals in pleasant, relaxing surroundings. Digestion is impeded by any emotional state, and conditions that might arouse such stress should be avoided.

## FOOD SUPPLEMENTS

Despite the zealous promotion of various food additives and dietary supplements by the producers of these products who advertise glowingly of improved physical performance due to their use, medical nutritionists continue to maintain that the manipulation of an already adequate diet will not improve performance:

In spite of occasional reports of apparently beneficial effects of vitamin supplementation upon athletic performance, it remains to be demonstrated convincingly that supplementation of the diet of the athlete in training with vitamins of any sort has a beneficial effect on endurance, muscular efficiency, or coordination.[1]

The claims of most commercial products offered as beneficial dietary additives are pseudoscientific at best. As Van Itallie and his co-researchers point out, "Manipulation of the diet in order to enhance physical performance is a procedure that has its roots in the superstitions and magic of the unrecorded past." [2]

A varied diet including green and yellow vegetables, citrus fruits, potatoes and other vegetables, dairy products, meat and eggs, breads and cereals, and

[1] Theodore B. Van Itallie, Leonardo Sinisterra, and Frederick J. Stare, "Nutrition and Athletic Performance," *Journal of the American Medical Association,* **162** (November 17, 1956), 1124.
[2] *Ibid.,* 1120.

fruits will provide all the vitamins needed by the body. Experts assure us that ". . . it is practically impossible for a normal healthy person living under ordinary circumstances to avoid the inclusion of adequate vitamins in his daily food intake." [3]

### SALT INTAKE

There is a great deal of misunderstanding on the part of coaches and trainees regarding the use of common table salt in the diet of the athlete. Salt is lost from the body through perspiration and urination, but this loss is replaced in the normal diet. Although it is common practice to prescribe enteric salt tablets for athletes in training and during competition, this practice often results in nausea and usually impairs digestion. The procedure is unnecessary and is not recommended. In the rare instances in which salt supplementation might be indicated (for example, during an *unusual* change in normal environmental temperature, resulting in extreme perspiration), this need is met most effectively through increased food salting.

As Klafs and Arnheim tell us "there is no evidence to support the common practice of increasing the salt intake of athletes in excess of the losses that accompany sweating in normal competitive situations." [4]

### PREMEET NUTRITION

Recent scientific studies indicate that specific pre-event nutrition should cover a period of some 48 hours prior to competition, rather than be limited merely to the traditional premeet meal. This expanded concept is based on research that has demonstrated that events calling for endurance can be beneficially affected by a maximum filling of carbohydrate stores.[5] This build-up of glycogen reserves requires about 48 hours and should be accompanied by a gradual decrease in energy output.

During this period, the carbohydrates in the diet should be increased by providing more breads, potatoes, sugar, and cereals. Fats (including whole milk) are not digested as readily as other foods even without the emotional stress inevitably present as competition approaches, and should be reduced or eliminated from the premeet nutrition.

The final meal prior to competition should consist of highly digestible foods that are familiar to the individual athlete, and the meal should be completed at least three hours before the meet. This period of time allows for adequate digestion and absorption of a carefully selected meal, without providing a delay lengthy enough to make the athlete hungry again.

[3] O. William Dayton, *Athletic Training and Conditioning* (New York: The Ronald Press Co., 1960), p. 33.
[4] Carl E. Klafs and Daniel D. Arnheim, *Modern Principles of Athletic Training* (St. Louis: The C. V. Mosby Company, 1963), p. 115.
[5] Van Itallie *et al., op. cit.,* 1125.

Athletes are often given sugar (honey, dextrose, or glucose) just prior to competition. This practice may result in some psychological benefit, but physiologically there is no evidence that it contributes to performance in the women's program of events. Such feeding does, however, lead to dehydration, and can result in severe gastric disturbances.[6] The practice is not recommended.

## WEIGHT CONTROL

In its simplest terms, weight control is merely a matter of adjusting energy intake and outgo. Body weight which remains constant indicates that the energy supplied by the food intake is balanced by the energy being used in regular bodily activity. A loss in weight results from an expenditure of energy greater than that provided by the diet, and an increase in weight means that the energy value of the food taken in is greater than the needs of the body.

The underweight person can gain weight only by increasing the energy intake (food) above the energy output (activity). This means that the amount of fats and other high calorie content food in the diet must be augmented. In the extreme cases, a reduction in physical activity is also indicated, but such a program is normally neither practical nor necessary in the case of girl athletes.

Overweight, which is the basic nutritional problem of American adults, results from an excess of energy intake over energy outgo. People who are overweight simply eat too much and exercise too little. To lose weight one must readjust the calorie difference by modifying the diet and increasing the regular amount of exercise.

Because athletes have a tendency to continue seasonal eating habits after the competitive season is over, a problem of many girls is that of weight gain during the off-season. When the exercise is decreased, the caloric intake must be decreased. During the off-season, girls should not vary far from their seasonal weight unless growth is still taking place.

## VEGETARIANISM

A vegetarian is a person who limits his diet to plant foods. There are few who comply with this rigid criterion (most "vegetarians" drink milk and eat eggs, for example), but there are some athletes who do not eat meat in any form. Since all food products, plant or animal, are converted into the same chemical compounds during the digestive process, the argument over the value of a vegetable (or a raw meat) diet as compared to a more normal one seems academic. The important factors are that the diet meets the nutritional needs of the body, that it is enjoyable, and that it maintains the weight of the athlete at a scheduled level.

[6] Klafs and Arnheim, *op. cit.*, p. 135.

## MENSTRUATION

Because of the importance of daily training in any serious athletic program, the menstrual period imposes problems due to the misunderstandings of this function on the part of many people. In the past, even medical practitioners advocated that girls and women should restrict exercise during menstruation, and although this concept is contradicted today, there is still a widespread lack of assurance on the part of many coaches and athletes as to the proper course of action relating to training and competition during this period. There is little published research on the relationship between athletic participation and the menstrual cycle, but a great deal of empirical evidence has accumulated indicating that regular and vigorous exercise has a beneficial effect on menstrual functions. In general, current medical opinion indicates that if the athlete is able to participate in the normal training routine or in athletic competition during her menstrual period without dysmenorrhea or other menstrual-related disturbances, there is no reason to discontinue or modify such activity.

A report that summarizes current medical opinion in this regard was published by the Research Committee of the DGWS in 1959.[7] The report was based on a survey of the opinions of eight gynecologists (chosen because of their special training) and nine women physicians (chosen because it was felt that their sex might provide further insights into the problem). Five of these seventeen doctors recommended "limited participation" in intensive sports competition during the first half of the menstrual period, but the other twelve physicians involved in the survey placed no restrictions at all on vigorous competitive sports participation during any phase of the menstrual cycle for those girls and women who are free from menstrual disturbances.[8]

As for the effect of menstruation on performance, Jokl reports a study presented at the 1952 Congress of Sports Medicine in Finland, which investigated this factor in a group of champion athletes in swimming, gymnastics, basketball, winter sports, and track and field. All but four of these women had participated in competition during the menstrual period without trouble of any sort. Twenty of the athletes claimed that their performances were improved during menstruation, 45 reported no noticeable effect on athletic efficiency, and 39 indicated that their performances were below normal.[9]

---

[7] Marjorie Phillips, Katherine Fox, and Olive Young. "Sports Activity for Girls," *JOHPER,* **30** (December, 1959), 23–25, 54.

[8] *Ibid.,* 24.

[9] Ernst Jokl, "La Situation Athlétique des Femmes," *Sport,* **22** (April, 1963), 110.

Jokl also reports that at the Melbourne Olympic Games in 1956, at least six gold medals were won in swimming and track and field by women during the menstrual period, and that apparently no contestants failed to compete in any event because of menstruation.[10]

## COMPETITIVE SEASON TRAINING

As mentioned previously, training for serious track and field participation must be a continuous effort. Throughout the year, sound nutrition, adequate rest, and a great deal of vigorous exercise must be combined with a psychological atmosphere concerned with the optimum welfare of the individual girl. Conditioning for high-level athletic performance in any sport is a long-range process. It cannot properly be hurried, and no attempt should be made to do so. The tempo of the conditioning emphasis should vary rather widely during the three loosely identified phases of the training year—the off-season, the preseason, and the competitive season.

The objective of the off-season (normally the summer months) is to maintain a relatively high level of fitness, but to do this through some activity other than track and field. This is a period of psychological refreshment, and the athlete will do well to develop new sports interests that will allow her to "forget" track and field until the fall.

The preseason begins in October or November and continues until the beginning of the competitive meets. This is the period of intensive conditioning. It is during these fall and winter months that the hard work which builds strength and endurance must be done.

After the competitive season is underway, the chief purpose of the training program is to maintain the high degree of condition that has been developed up to this point, and to get the athlete to each meet in the best possible condition of physical and psychological readiness.

During this phase of the training program, emphasis is placed on competition rather than on conditioning, and the hard exertion involved in the strength and endurance building programs of the preseason is reduced to the minimum necessary to maintain peak fitness. Practice sessions are made up largely of a refining of techniques. Normally, hard work is limited to one day early in each week, and the workouts of the two days prior to a meet usually consist merely of limbering exercises.

[10] Jokl, *op. cit.*

# 3

# Who's Fastest?

## BACKGROUND

Swiftness of foot had basic survival value among our primitive ancestors, and the concept of this ability to overtake a fleeing enemy or a potential meal, or to escape from an inherently dangerous situation involving man or animal, gradually became embodied in sporting contests measuring one man's speed against a rival's. Such early competitive contests were short races, favoring the sprinter over the runner with greater endurance, largely because the extended period of training required by the longer races made such events impractical for the typical challenge-type foot races of primitive, pioneer, or rural societies.

As far as we know from recorded history, the earliest organized track competition for women took place in ancient Greece. Women were barred from the Olympic Games, but Pausanias, Greek chronicler of the second century A.D., tells us that they had their own festival at Olympia, the *Heraea*, at which foot races were held for unmarried girls in three age-group classifications.[1] The girl sprinters competed in the Olympic stadium, but did not run the full *stade* race of the men. As Pausanias indicates, "the course of the stadium is shortened for them by about one-sixth of its length," [2] making the distance of the girls' races approximately 165 yards. We do not know when such events began, but our second century reporter observes: "The games of the maidens too are traced back to ancient times." [3]

The first international meet of modern times, the Monte Carlo Games of 1921, included a 60-meter dash and a longer race—which perhaps was considered a middle distance event—of 250 meters. Both contests were won by Mary Lines, one of Britain's all-time great sprinters.

[1] Pausanias, *Descriptions of Greece,* trans. W. H. S. Jones and H. A. Ormerod, Vol. II (London: William Heinemann, Ltd., 1926), p. 473.
[2] *Ibid.*
[3] *Ibid.*

Sprints were the only running events, other than a hurdles race and a relay, on the program of the first national AAU meet for women. Both a 50-yard and a 100-yard dash were included, and the first champion sprinters were Marion McCartie, who clocked :06.6 in winning the 50, and Frances Ruppert, whose :12.0 won her the gold medal in the 100. Thus began an early American concentration on the dashes that has continued to this day. Interestingly enough, short sprinting has been the only track and field activity in which our women consistently have achieved any real degree of success in international competition.

In the first ten Olympic Games in which women participated, United States entries have been gold medal winners in the 100-meter event on five occasions, and only in 1948 did our girls fail to place in the top six:

| | | |
|---|---|---|
| Amsterdam (1928) | Elizabeth Robinson | First |
| Los Angeles (1932) | Wilhelmina Von Bremen | Third |
| | Elizabeth Wilde | Sixth |
| Berlin (1936) | Helen Stephens | First |
| | Annette Rogers | Fifth |
| London (1948) | | (failed to place) |
| Helsinki (1952) | Mae Faggs | Sixth |
| Melbourne (1956) | Isabelle Daniels | Fourth |
| Rome (1960) | Wilma Rudolph | First |
| Tokyo (1964) | Wyomia Tyus | First |
| | Edith McGuire | Second |
| | Marilyn White | Fourth |
| Mexico City (1968) | Wyomia Tyus | First |
| | Barbara Ferrell | Second |
| | Margaret Bailes | Fifth |
| Munich (1972) | Iris Davis | Fourth |

American sprinters have not been as successful in the 200-meter run. Rudolph won this event at the Rome Olympics and McGuire at Tokyo, but our only other places in this event have been Audrey Patterson's third at London in 1948, and Ferrell's fourth and Tyus' sixth at Mexico City in 1968.

The 220-yard dash was added to the AAU program in 1926, and the first national championship in this event was won by Frances Keddie with a time of :28.6.

Olympic champions in the sprints to date include:

*100-Meter Dash*

| | | |
|---|---|---|
| 1928 | Elizabeth Robinson (United States) | :12.2 |
| 1932 | Stanislawa Walasiewicz (Poland) | :11.9 |
| 1936 | Helen Stephens (United States) | :11.5 |
| 1948 | Francina Blankers-Koen (Netherlands) | :11.9 |
| 1952 | Marjorie Jackson (Australia) | :11.5 |
| 1956 | Betty Cuthbert (Australia) | :11.5 |
| 1960 | Wilma Rudolph (United States) | :11.0 |
| 1964 | Wyomia Tyus (United States) | :11.4 |
| 1968 | Wyomia Tyus (United States) | :11.0 |
| 1972 | Renate Stecher (East Germany) | :11.1 |

*200-Meter Dash*

| 1948 | Francina Blankers-Koen (Netherlands) | :24.4 |
| 1952 | Marjorie Jackson (Australia) | :23.7 |
| 1956 | Betty Cuthbert (Australia) | :23.4 |
| 1960 | Wilma Rudolph (United States) | :24.0 |
| 1964 | Edith McGuire (United States) | :23.0 |
| 1968 | Irena Kirszenstein (Poland) | :22.5 |
| 1972 | Renate Stecher (East Germany) | :22.4 |

## NATURE OF THE EVENTS

Traditionally, these track events include all running distances of 220 yards or less. By its very definition, sprinting is a speed-contest, and sheer running speed is primarily the result of characteristics which are innate. Although the total effort involved in successful sprinting performance is a very complex combination of many intricate factors, perhaps largely environmental, the potential for fast running is a characteristic that a girl either has or does not have. Speed, *per se,* is not something that can be developed. Through dedicated practice in improving techniques and in building power, however, any runner can become faster. This apparent paradox is based on two facts:

(1) Learned skills are more efficient than trial-and-error attempts to perform the same movements, and thus any refined (that is, practiced) specific action will be executed in a shorter period of time than will an unlearned effort to perform the same exercise. Practice does not make perfect, but even an error can be perfected through practice!

(2) The most important factor in any athletic activity is power. This is a term that represents a rather complex concept, but basically power is a combination of strength and speed of muscular reaction. The latter element is something that we can't do much about, but strength is readily improved and more strength means more power. Power, again, is a factor which makes the athlete "faster."

Nevertheless, despite the fact that a runner can become faster, the top-notch sprinter is born with most of the characteristics that classify her in this category, and all coaches are, at least subconsciously, always on the look-out for girls with the exceedingly rare combination of physical, mental, and emotional traits that is basic to the makeup of the natural sprinter.

Body type does not prove as helpful in spotting potential sprinters as it does with many other athletic events. Champion sprinters have been tall, short, stocky, lean—and every conceivable combination of these variables. Fortunately, however, there are a few recognizable characteristics that offer aid to the coach in locating the fast runners. Since the sprinter type has short reaction and reflex times, she usually exhibits rather typical mannerisms. The fast girl is alert, restless, vigorous, and quick of movement; the distinguishing mark of this type is a spirited temperament. Like the race horse, the sprinter is high-strung. Another hint is that the girl with sprinting ability is usually aware of this advantage, even though its relation to track and field athletics may not have occurred to her. She is the one who has been able to outrun her contemporaries all through childhood, and who, as a youngster, was usually a standout in games of low organization simply because she was quicker than others in her age-group. Even when the fast girl does not recognize her ability, her immediate friends will know of it, and a few judicious questions directed toward student leaders in any school group will frequently provide the teacher or coach with a great deal of information regarding the speed, and other exceptional physical abilities, of various members of the student body.

A more precise means of ferreting out sprinters among any group of youngsters is to run them through a 50-yard or 75-yard dash test. Since a testing setup is a vital part of any good physical education program, the addition of a sprint item to the regular test battery should be a simple procedure in most school situations.

DGWS rules classify sprinting events as follows:

| Elementary (grades 4–6) | Junior High School (grades 7–9) | Senior High School (grades 10–12) | College and Open |
|---|---|---|---|
| 50 yards | 50 yards | 50 yards | 100 yards |
| 75 yards | 100 yards | 100 yards | 220 yards |
| 100 yards | 220 yards | 220 yards | |
| 220 yards | | | |

AAU rules provide slightly different groupings:

| Age-Group (age 9 and under) | Age-Group (age 10 and 11) | Age-Group (age 12 and 13) | Girls' Competition (age 14–17) | Women's Competition (age 14 or older) |
|---|---|---|---|---|
| 50 yards | 50 yards | 50 yards | 50 yards | 50 yards– 60 meters |
| 100 yards | 100 yards | 100 yards | 100 yards | 100 yards–100 meters |
| 220 yards | 220 yards | 220 yards | 220 yards | 220 yards–200 meters |

Sprinting events shorter than 220 yards or 200 meters are normally run on a straight course. AAU rules require the 200 meters (or 220 yards) to be run around one turn, and this race also should be run in this manner in meets conducted by schools or other agencies besides the AAU in order to conform to international regulations.

## SPRINTING TECHNIQUE

In any consideration of performance technique, a preliminary understanding must be that there are many ways of doing a thing "right." *Any* way that produces better performance for a particular athlete is the best way for her. In working with sprinters, in particular, the coach must remember that the only real test of ability is measured by the stop watch, not by some aesthetic judgment of which form looks best, or some evaluation of which technique most closely follows currently approved practices. The many successfully employed variations in running styles underline this point. On the other hand, there are general mechanical and biological principles which apply to any motor activity and for such efforts to be effective, idiosyncrasies of style must be within limitations imposed by physics and physiology.

## MECHANICS OF RUNNING

Women have a mechanical disadvantage in running, compared to men, because of the wider pelvis and the resulting obliquity of the femur. This anatomical difference results in a sideways shift of the center of gravity with each stride, and most women run with a pronounced lateral sway of the pelvis. Attempts to compensate for this action often lead to inefficient and awkward movement patterns. The most common compensation is an outward throw of the lower leg and foot during the forward movement of each stride. This rotates the femur inward, and the reaction to this effect is a twisting motion of the trunk with each stride. Another frequently found error resulting from the attempt of women to compensate for lateral sway is a fixed position of the upper arms against the sides, and an outward throwing motion of the lower arms from the elbows. To reduce these running disadvantages, teaching emphasis should be placed on a high, straightforward knee lift, and a correct arm action.

Running involves a somewhat complicated coordination in which the body is moved forward by a pushing action of the back leg. The result is a series of bounding motions more or less tied together, and the effectiveness of the total effort is determined largely by the smoothness with which these bounds are coordinated.

The feet strike the ground with just enough lateral spread to maintain adequate balance—experienced runners run almost on a line—and the toes should be pointed straight ahead. Toeing in or toeing out is a mechanical error which reduces the efficiency of running.

The arms swing in opposition to the leg action, serving as a balancing force that keeps the body aligned in the direction of travel. The arms are swung obliquely across the body from a mid-torso position to a point slightly outside of and even with the hips. In all types of running, from sprinting to cross-country, the hands should be held naturally with the fingers loosely curled.

In sprinting, the body should have a definite forward lean. The amount of this inclination will vary among sprinters, and depends to a large extent upon the individual's leg strength. Usually this angle varies between 20 to 25 degrees, but Doherty suggests that a forward lean of as much as 35 degrees may be possible, and indicates that the achievement of such a running position can be an important factor in lowering present sprinting records.[4]

## STARTING

The advantage of an initial low body position in increasing the driving force exerted through the forceful extension of the front leg is obvious, and the crouch start technique is used the world over by experienced sprinters.

The major variations in starting practices between different sprinters are in the spacing between starting blocks, and in the elevation of the hips in the "set" position. In spite of the wide range of these differences, however, research subsequent to World War II has indicated that the so-called medium start and a moderate hip height are the most effective techniques in terms of the sprinter's elapsed time at 10 yards and at 50 yards.

The first problem in learning to use the crouch start is to determine the optimum measurements from the back of the starting line to the front edge of the front block, and between the front and back starting blocks. These spacings are individually established by having each novice runner assume a comfortable "on your mark" position (without using blocks) in which the weight of the body rests on the ball of the left foot and the knee of the right leg. The knee on the ground should be about an inch forward of the toe of the opposite foot. From this position, the girl raises her hips to an elevation slightly higher than her shoulders, and then adjusts her hands forward or backward until the body weight is supported largely on the hands, but with enough weight on the forward leg so that there is no undue arm discomfort in maintaining this attitude for 5 or 6 seconds. In most cases, from the side view the arms will be at right angles to the track surface in the correct "set" position. While the sprinter is holding this attitude, the coach or a teammate scratches marks on the ground just forward of the hands, and at the toe of each foot. The measured distances between these scratch marks are then used as base spacings for the placement of starting blocks. Slight adjustments may be necessary when an actual starting line and blocks are used, but such modifications will be minor and easily made.

### "ON YOUR MARKS"

The recommended initial starting position is illustrated in Fig. 7. In taking this position the runner stands just behind the starting line, feet

[4] Kenneth Doherty, *Modern Track and Field* (2d ed.); Englewood Cliffs, N. J.: Prentice-Hall, Inc., 1963, p. 83.

straddling the longitudinal axis of the starting blocks, and at the command, "on your marks," bends forward at the waist and places her hands on the ground several inches in front of the starting line. From this position the lead foot is carefully placed in the front block, making sure that the entire sole is exerting firm pressure on the block face and that the toe of the shoe is just touching the ground. The back foot is then placed with the same care on the rear block, and the knee of this leg is allowed to settle to the track, comfortably supporting the body weight. The hands are next moved to a position on the ground immediately behind the starting line. Most sprinters place their hands slightly more than shoulder width apart. The wrists are rotated inward so that the thumbs point toward each other and the thumbs and forefingers parallel the starting line. The fingers are bridged, forming a tripod-like base with each hand.

The sprinter is under no compulsion to rush in assuming this initial starting position. The starter will give each girl in a race ample time to acquire exactly the position she desires. No competitor, however, will be allowed to delay or extend the making of minor body adjustments to a degree that might handicap the other runners. From the beginning of their training, athletes should be coached to assume the starting position

**Fig. 7.** Recommended position at the initial starting command, "on your marks."

deliberately, but without undue delay, immediately upon the command, "on your marks."

When the runner is ready she signifies this condition to the starter by becoming motionless. In this attitude, it is important that the position of the head be comfortable. The runner should avoid holding the head up in a neck-cramping position, but she should also avoid the opposite extreme of a blind, chin-on-chest head carry that may impede orientation at the start of the race. The optimum position is achieved by focusing the eyes downward toward a spot on the track about 2 feet in front of the starting line.

**Fig. 8.** Recommended position at the secondary starting command, "set."

## "SET"

When all of the runners are motionless, the starter will give the second preparatory command, "set." At this signal, the girl raises her hips to an elevation slightly higher than her shoulders (see Fig. 8), and concentrates her attention on reacting to the imminent sound of the gun.

## "GO!"

At the sound of the starting signal, the sprinter should drive hard against both blocks, but, obviously, the front leg is the important driving force simply because this foot pushes on the block until the leg is completely

**Fig. 9.** First stride from the blocks. Note front (left) leg drive and forceful compensating arm swing.

extended. Forward progress is initiated with a strong, forward movement of the rear leg, accompanied by a forceful, compensating swing of the arms (see Fig. 9). The arm swing is a natural reflex pattern, and at the start is more vigorous than in full stride running in order to balance the forceful leg drive. During the first few strides, the arms should move obliquely across the body from a shoulder-high position at the sternum to a point 6 inches behind and outside of the hips.

The body position is kept low to take full advantage of the horizontal component of the leg drive, and to maintain this lean without loss of balance the first strides are relatively short. Stride length is a natural reaction, though, and the novice should concentrate on the forward lean and not attempt to chop her stride. The stride will adjust to the necessities of the body angle. This angle gradually reduces itself during the first few strides until the sprinter is in her normal running position with a body lean of some 20 to 25 degrees.

## FINISHING

The finish of a sprint or any other distance should be no different from the normal, controlled stride pattern the athlete uses during the final 10 to 15 yards of the race. Many contests have been won by the second best runner, though, simply because of a tendency for the front runner to ease up just prior to reaching the finish line! The novice athlete in training must be impressed with the necessity of running through the tape. The "finish line" habitually should be thought of as being several strides beyond the tape.

COMPARATIVE TYPICAL PERFORMANCES

| Sprinting Events | Physical Education Classes. | | Competitive | | | |
|---|---|---|---|---|---|---|
| | High School | College | High School | College | National Class | International Class |
| 50 yards (45.72 m) | :08.3 | :08.5 | :07.0 | :07.0 | — | — |
| 100 yards (91.44 m) | :13.4 | :13.5 | :12.0 | :12.0 | :11.0 | :10.6 |
| 100 meters (109 yds., 1 ft. 1 in.) | :14.8 | :14.9 | :13.2 | :13.2 | :12.0 | :11.6 |
| 220 yards (201.17 m) | :33.3 | :35.3 | :27.0 | :29.0 | :24.9 | :23.8 |
| 200 meters (218 yds., 2 ft. 2 in.) | :33.0 | :35.0 | :26.8 | :28.8 | :24.7 | :23.6 |

# 4

# Hurdling Is Artistic Sprinting

## BACKGROUND

Hurdle races have been contested in women's meets since the first inter-national competition. Included in the program of the Monte Carlo Games of 1921 were two events which, assuming that they were both run over the same height hurdles, seem practically duplicates. One race at this meet was a 74-meter event and the other was listed as 63 meters! Unusual, too—from a 40-year-later point of view—were the racing distances. As a matter of fact, there was an almost chaotic lack of standardization regarding the length of these events in the early meets. Until about 1930, programs included such various hurdling races as: 50 yards, 60 yards, 100 yards, 120 yards, 60 meters, 63 meters, 74 meters, 80 meters, 83 meters, and 100 meters!

In the First Women's Olympic Games at Paris in 1922, a 100-yard hurdles race was on the program, and this same event was included in the Second Women's World Games, held in 1926 at Göteborg. By the time of the third running of the Women's Games, however, the 80-meter race had become the standard, and hurdling was introduced as an official Olympic event at this distance in 1932 at Los Angeles. For the next 36 years—through the Mexico City Olympiad—although a variety of running distances were still contested, the standard women's hurdle event, the world over, was an 80-meter race.

Until 1969, a 30-inch hurdle was used for all women's events, irrespective of the distance of the course. Beginning with that year, the 80-meter race was replaced in the program by a 100-meter event, and, for AAU and inter-national competition, the hurdle height was increased for all races of less than 200 meters.

The fabulous Mildred Didrikson was the first Olympic champion, with teammate Evelyne Hall taking second place. Simone Schaller, the third American entry, placed fourth in this race for the most successful United States showing in women's international track and field sports to the present

41

day. In hurdling competition from 1932 through 1972, as a matter of fact, only two other Americans—Rosie Bonds at Tokyo and Pat Van Wolvelaere at Mexico City—ever reached an Olympic Games final round.

Olympic champions in the hurdles to date include:

*80 Meters*

| | | |
|---|---|---|
| 1932 | Mildred Didrikson (United States) | :11.7 |
| 1936 | Trebisonda Valla (Italy) | :11.7 |
| 1948 | Francina Blankers-Koen (Netherlands) | :11.2 |
| 1952 | Shirley Strickland de la Hunty (Australia) | :10.9 |
| 1956 | Shirley Strickland de la Hunty (Australia) | :10.7 |
| 1960 | Irina Press (U.S.S.R.) | :10.8 |
| 1964 | Karin Balzer (East Germany) | :10.5 |
| 1968 | Maureen Caird (Australia) | :10.3 |

*100 Meters*

| | | |
|---|---|---|
| 1972 | Annelie Ehrhardt (East Germany) | :12.6 |

## NATURE OF THE EVENTS

Women's hurdle races are run over barriers either 33 inches or 30 inches high. The 33-inch height is standard for all international racing distances under 200 meters, and is used with a spacing of 27 feet 10½ inches between hurdles. The 30-inch hurdles are used in the women's 200-meter and 400-meter races.

The 30-inch hurdle height is standard for all DGWS events except the 100-meter race in which the 33-inch hurdle is used.

DGWS classifications include the following hurdle events:

| Elementary (grades 4–6) | Junior High School (grades 7–9) | Senior High School (grades 10–12) | College and Open |
|---|---|---|---|
| 50 yards | 50 yards | 50 yards | 80 yards |
| | 80 yards | 80 yards | 100 meters |
| | | 100 meters | 200 meters |
| | | 200 meters | |

The AAU does not include a hurdles event in the two lower divisions of their age-group program, and only the 50-yard event in the other two classifications below open competition:

| Age-Group (age 9 and under) | Age-Group (age 10 and 11) | Age-Group (age 12 and 13) | Girls' Competition (age 14–17) | Women's Competition (age 14 or older) |
|---|---|---|---|---|
| (no event) | (no event) | 50 yards | 50 yards | 50 yards |
| | | | 100 meters | 60 yards |
| | | | 400 meters | 70 yards |
| | | | | 100 meters |
| | | | | 200 meters |
| | | | | 400 meters |

Since running over 30- and 33-inch barriers is more closely allied to the sprints than to a real hurdling event (such as the men's high hurdles), competitors in the women's events must have many of the same characteristics that lead to successful performance in the dashes.  Candidates for the hurdles should, first of all, be fast, and, as indicated previously, this enviable trait is one which unfortunately cannot be acquired except through the vagaries of heredity.  Two factors, in particular, that contribute to the complex speed characteristic are essential in the makeup of the hurdler—short reaction time and short reflex time.  Without these traits, no one will achieve top-notch performance in the hurdles.

A second characteristic of the successful hurdler is a calculated disregard for the possibility of physical pain resulting from hitting hurdles.  Any obstacle which must be jumped over always poses a psychological hazard.  In running a flight of hurdles there is always the possibility that the runner may not clear the next barrier, and this possibility is of some very real concern to the athlete.  Errors of judgment invariably result in more or less serious contusions, and they can result in extremely grave injuries.  Whatever the degree of seriousness of such accident, they all hurt!  The novice hurdler is going to get bumps, and even experts are not immune.  Nevertheless, a runner who consciously or subconsciously fears the anticipated knocks will never be a winning hurdler.  Hurdling demands courage of the kind with which a girl can put these inevitable bruises out of her mind.

While body size and physique are not vitally significant factors in running the women's hurdles events, the girl with longer legs has certain innate mechanical advantages over the shorter hurdler.  Generally speaking, however, as with any sprinting event, top-flight competitors come in all shapes and sizes.  Again, speed and courage are the basic requirements.  A girl with these traits who also is willing to work hard and to sacrifice a great many short-range material things in the pursuit of excellence is a most likely candidate for the hurdling events.

## PRELIMINARY TRAINING

The coach of the girl who wants to learn to hurdle should aim to have her student achieve two important goals almost from the outset of her training.  First, the hurdler should make rapid and self-apparent progress, avoiding the psychological blocks of fear and/or failure; and, second, she must perceive that the technique of clearing the hurdle is simply a modified running stride.  A method of achieving these two objectives that has proved very successful is to start the girl running over a 12-inch "hurdle" assembled from makeshift standards (building blocks and bricks make excellent standards for this purpose) and a wood dowel, a length of discarded high jump crossbar, or a piece of aluminum tubing (see Fig. 10).  Over a period

**Fig. 10.** A simple apparatus used at Florida State University for teaching hurdling techniques to beginners.

of several practice sessions the height of the crossbar is gradually raised until the novice is clearing the standard 30 or 33 inches. The concept involved in this procedure is that with the low introduction to hurdling the girl will have no insecurity regarding her ability to clear the barrier from the first attempt—she will almost assuredly begin with success—and that even if she does inadvertently strike and dislodge the crossbar during her repeated tries at gradually increasing heights, any such miscues in all probability will be painless.

Success in the initial efforts at a new skill and the avoidance of pain during its execution provide ego satisfaction, assurance that the task is within one's ability, and a challenge to try the next step—conditions that are characteristic of the most efficient learning situations.

As the height of the training crossbar is raised, the girl should be introduced to the actual hurdling skills. Although the technique of clearing a hurdle is basically a running stride, the modifications required for efficiency make the action one of considerable complexity, and as soon as the student begins to gain confidence in her ability to run over an 18- or 20-inch hurdle she should begin working on the unusual movement pattern involved in the total hurdling effort. This coordination, incidentally, calls for a high degree of flexibility, and stretching and bending calisthenics must become an important part of each day's training for the hurdler. Extreme suppleness is an essential characteristic for successful hurdling.

## HURDLING TECHNIQUE

The hurdling stride is started by kicking up the lead led with a high knee action, as though the thigh were to be placed against the chest (see Fig. 11a). This fast swing-up must be in a straight-ahead line, and the whole

(a) Takeoff. Note distance from hurdle.

**Fig. 11.** Hurdling form.

leg action, in relation to the hurdle, should be a smooth, continuous up, over, and down movement. The lead leg does not go up *and then* down. Experienced hurdlers think of the motion as a flowing uninterrupted trajectory over the hurdle.

As the lead knee is lifted, the forward lean of the upper body is increased. If, as suggested above, the hurdler thinks of lifting the upper leg to the chest, she should also think of this lean as a movement in which she pulls her chest down to meet the leg. This forward bend from the hips is accompanied by a forward thrust of the arm and shoulder opposite the lead leg, which has the essential purpose of keeping the shoulders square with the running direction in order to maintain balance and orientation upon landing.

The takeoff leg should follow the lead leg smoothly and with increasing acceleration. A common fault of beginners is to float motionlessly over the hurdle with the back leg trailing behind, from takeoff to landing, like the tail of a kite. Actually, the upper part of the rear leg begins to move forward as soon as the takeoff foot leaves the ground, but the movement is unhurried initially, and is limited to the thigh. As this part of the leg moves forward, it is lifted to the side and pulled through with a knee lead in a sweeping motion (see Fig. 11b). The rear leg does not clear the hurdle until after the center of gravity of the body has done so. Throughout this action, the lower leg trails, extending backward from the flexed knee which is lifted high enough to the side to clear the top bar. During the forward sweep of the thigh over the bar, the ankle is rotated, turning the foot outward to prevent it from hooking the hurdle top.

As the lead leg goes over the hurdle on its downward trajectory, the pull-through of the rear leg is accelerated, and with a continued high knee action this leg finally catches and moves past the landing leg, becoming the new lead leg of the first stride after the hurdle (see Fig. 11c).

(b) Clearance. Note trailing leg position, body lean, and compensating arm action.

**Fig. 11. Continued.**

(c) Touch-down. Note trailing leg–knee position.

**Fig. 11.** *Continued.*

The body forward lean which is accentuated at the takeoff is maintained throughout the hurdle clearance, and as the lead foot lands and the now fast-moving takeoff leg continues through on the next stride, the action should flow into a balanced, full-stride sprinting form without any break or hesitation in the runner's momentum.

Since hurdling is simply a modified and extended running stride, arm action is in normal opposition to the legs throughout the movement. The only modification is in the accentuated thrust of the arm opposite the lead leg at takeoff, necessary to keep the upper body from twisting due to the extended stride.

## THE START

Hurdlers should start and run their events as though they were flat sprint races. Starting form and body action to the first hurdle are both exactly similar to sprinting techniques.

Top-flight hurdlers normally use seven strides in covering the distance from the starting line to the first hurdle in all events shorter than the 200-meter race, but small girls or beginners probably will find it necessary to use eight strides. In either case, the athlete must reach the hurdle—that is, must complete the seven or eight strides—on her takeoff foot. If the forward lead leg is the right one (that is, a left foot takeoff), a seven-stride approach will require that the hurdler start with her right foot in the forward block. An eight-stride approach will consequently require a left foot forward starting position. If the hurdler favors a left leg lead, these starting positions must then be reversed.

In the hurdles events which are run on a straightaway, there is no advantage in taking off from a particular leg. In curve running, however, such as in races of 200 meters or longer, a right takeoff leg is obviously a decided advantage in maintaining balance. A few beginners will be able to hurdle from either leg, but most athletes find it more natural to do any springing, jumping, or hurdling from a preferred leg—usually the left.

The distance of the takeoff from the front of the hurdle will vary with different runners, but for the girl of average size it will generally be about 5½ feet.

## THE HURDLES RACES

In all of the women's events, unless the hurdler can effectively alternate her takeoff leg, the distance between barriers must be covered in an odd number of strides. Unfortunately, many girls cannot master this rather complex skill, and, for those who would like to compete in the shorter hurdles races, *three* strides is the only efficient choice. As previously indicated, these strides should be part of an all-out sprinting effort. Hurdle races should be run as though the barriers were not there, and the development of such an attitude requires a great deal of running over *flights* of hurdles. One common mistake of beginners is that of devoting a disproportionate amount of their practice time to running repeatedly over a single hurdle. The hurdling effort is a complex, interrelated pattern of which the part of the race after the first hurdle is the significant fraction. Hurdlers should do most of their practice over flights of no fewer than three hurdles.

Most beginning hurdlers emphasize acceleration up to the first hurdle, but then settle into a striding continuation of the speed developed to that point until the final hurdle is cleared. This unfortunate habit evolves from the necessity of stressing the rhythmic three-stride pattern between hurdles during the technique-learning process. This inclination is one that the girl with a desire to be a winner must avoid. Research points out that maximum velocity is not reached in a sprinting effort until about 6 seconds after the start. This means that in a women's hurdle race, acceleration can continue up to and beyond the third hurdle. Runners should be indoctrinated with the concept of continuing the effort to increase their velocity to the point of top speed regardless of intervening hurdles.

After clearing the final hurdle, the runner should concentrate her efforts on finishing under good control. As in any race, the all-out driving effort should be continued to a point several yards beyond the final tape.

### COMPARATIVE TYPICAL PERFORMANCES

| Hurdling Events | Physical Education Classes | | Competitive | | | |
| --- | --- | --- | --- | --- | --- | --- |
| | High School | College | High School | College | National Class | International Class |
| 50 yards (45.72 m) | :10.4 | :10.5 | :07.3 | :07.4 | — | — |
| 100 meters (109 yds., 1 ft. 1 in.) | — | — | :16.5 | :16.5 | :15.3 | :14.0 |
| 200 meters (218 yds., 2 ft. 2 in.) | — | — | :31.5 | :31.5 | :29.6 | :27.8 |
| 400 meters (437 yds., 1 ft. 4 in.) | — | — | — | — | 1:06 | 1:02 |

# 5

# The Team Effort Called Relays

## BACKGROUND

According to Doherty, relay racing as a competitive sport originated in the United States, and relay racing as a specific track and field event had its start at the University of Pennsylvania in 1893.[1]

In women's meets, relay races have been included since the beginning of such contests. The British Inter-Services Championships of 1919 included a 440-yard relay for women of the military services, and the pioneer international meet for women, the Monte Carlo Games of 1921, scheduled two relays—300 meters (4 × 75 meters) and 800 meters (4 × 200 meters).

A Philadelphia Meadowbrook Club team composed of Frances Ruppert, Dorothy Bough, Grace Ritter, and Madeline Adams won the first national 440-yard relay championship in the first women's AAU meet of 1923, with a time of :52.4.

For some obscure reason, although American girls have seldom crowded the lists of world-class performances in track and field events, they have tended to monopolize the 400-meter relay as though it were United States property. In the first ten Olympic Games in which this event has been held, our sprint relay teams failed to win medals only at London in 1948 and at Munich in 1972:

| | | |
|---|---|---|
| Amsterdam (1928) | Mary Washburn, Jessie Cross, Loretta McNeill, and Elizabeth Robinson | Second |
| Los Angeles (1932) | Mary Carew, Evelyn Furtsch, Annette Rogers, and Wilhelmina Von Bremen | First |
| Berlin (1936) | Harriet Blan, Annette Rogers, Elizabeth Robinson, and Helen Stephens | First |
| London (1948) | | (failed to place) |
| Helsinki (1952) | Mae Faggs, Barbara Jones, Janet Moreau, and Catherine Hardy | First |

[1] Doherty, *op. cit.*, pp. 255–56.

| Melbourne (1956) | Mae Faggs, Margaret Mathews, Wilma Rudolph, and Isabelle Daniels | Third |
| Rome (1960) | Martha Hudson, Barbara Jones, Lucinda Williams, and Wilma Rudolph | First |
| Tokyo (1964) | Willye White, Wyomia Tyus, Marilyn White, and Edith McGuire | Second |
| Mexico City (1968) | Barbara Ferrell, Margaret Bailes, Mildrette Netter, and Wyomia Tyus | First |
| Munich (1972) | Martha Watson, Mattline Render, Mildrette Netter, and Iris Davis | Fourth |

The 1600-meter relay was added to the program at Munich, and the American girls wasted no time in adapting this event to the pattern by winning the silver medal.

Olympic champions in the relays to date include:

### 400-Meter Relay

| | | |
|---|---|---|
| 1928 | Canada | :48.4 |
| 1932 | United States | :47.0 |
| 1936 | United States | :46.9 |
| 1948 | Netherlands | :47.5 |
| 1952 | United States | :45.9 |
| 1956 | Australia | :44.5 |
| 1960 | United States | :44.5 |
| 1964 | Poland | :43.6 |
| 1968 | United States | :42.8 |
| 1972 | West Germany | :42.8 |

### 1600-Meter Relay

| | | |
|---|---|---|
| 1972 | East Germany | 3:23.0 |

## NATURE OF THE EVENTS

Relay races are team contests in which teammates (usually four) each run specified fractions of the total distance of the race. Two forms of relay races are recognized—pursuit and shuttle. In the pursuit relay, teammates run in the same direction, and each runner must pass a baton to the succeeding runner within a passing zone 10 meters on either side of the starting line for each relay leg. Shuttle relays are those in which alternate teammates run in opposite directions. Instead of passing a baton, the starting signal is given by each runner to his succeeding teammate by a touch on the right shoulder as he completes his leg of the race.

Although shuttle relays are often interesting, they can become extremely confusing to spectators and judges alike if the field spreads out significantly. Invariably they require more organization, more officials, and more know-how to conduct than do the more commonly run pursuit races.

Some pursuit races are called medley relays. These are events in which teammates run different length legs of the race, rather than the more conventional practice of having each member of a team run the same distance.

In the early days of relay racing, a flag, or some other conspicuous object, was passed from one runner to the next at the end of each leg. This procedure evolved into a hand touch-off that is still the accepted form in children's relay games, as well as in standard shuttle races. The baton pass was introduced as a necessary compromise between the early, unwieldy flag and the unreliability of judging the legality of touch-offs.

The official baton is a smooth hollow tube made of wood, paper composition, or metal, not longer than 300 millimeters (11.81 inches), with a circumference of 120 millimeters (4.72 inches) and a weight not less than 50 grams (1.76 ounces).

In an attempt to provide more girls with competitive track and field opportunities, the DGWS has recognized an amazing array of relay events in their four grade classifications:

| Elementary (grades 4–6) | Junior High School (grades 7–9) | Senior High School (grades 10–12) | College and Open |
|---|---|---|---|
| 220-yard pursuit | 220-yard pursuit | 440-yard pursuit | 440-yard pursuit |
| 220-yard shuttle | 440-yard pursuit | 880-yard pursuit | 880-yard pursuit |
| 440-yard pursuit | 880-yard pursuit | One mile pursuit | One mile pursuit |
|  | 880-yard pursuit medley (200, 110, 110, 440) | 880-yard pursuit medley (200, 110, 110, 440) | 880-yard pursuit medley (200, 110, 110, 440) |

AAU rules include the following events:

| Age-Group (age 9 and under) | Age-Group (age 10 and 11) and Age-Group (age 12 and 13) | Girls' Competition (age 14–17) | Women's Competition (age 14 or older) |
|---|---|---|---|
| 440-yard pursuit | 440-yard pursuit | 440-yard pursuit | 440-yard (400 meters) pursuit |
| 880-yard pursuit | 880-yard pursuit medley (220, 110, 110, 440) | 880-yard pursuit | 880-yard (800 meters) pursuit) |
|  |  | One mile pursuit | One mile (1600 meters) pursuit |
|  |  | 880-yard pursuit medley (220, 110, 110, 440) | Two-mile (3200 meters) pursuit |
|  |  |  | 880-yard (800 meters) pursuit medley (220, 110, 110, 440) (200, 100, 100, 400) |

## THE BATON EXCHANGE

The secret of winning relay teams is invariably closely associated with the group's skill in passing the baton. Since several seconds can be lost at each of these exchanges, it is not uncommon for a team to be beaten by slower runners who possess superior technique in the exchange zone.

The basic concept upon which efficient baton handling must be founded is that of naturalness. Since the primary objective in the relay events is to

run a race, a secondary motor skill—which must be performed as an incre-
ment to, and without detracting from, the major purpose—should prove
effective to the degree that the best running position is maintained during
its execution. Many of the popular styles of baton passing ignore this
seemingly rather apparent observation, and awkward, slow passes are
commonplace in most relay events.

A subordinate maxim is that the exchange techniques must be practiced
repeatedly. Too many coaches fail to budget available practice time in
such a way that drills on relay passing are scheduled regularly and frequently. Repetitive effort is essential in cutting important seconds from
the time consumed in each exchange zone.

Two baton transfer techniques are considered in this chapter—the sprint
exchange and the standard exchange. With both styles it is recommended
that the form known as the *inside pass* be used. With the inside pass the
baton is carried in the right hand and received in the left, and the exchange
is made on the left side (curb side) of the receiving runner. Although
there is no particular advantage to the inside pass with the sprint exchange,
there is a significant benefit when it is used with the standard exchange,
and it is recommended that the baton *always* be carried in the right hand
and received in the left, in order to avoid confusion.

## THE SPRINT PASS

Since most women's relay events are composed of sprint legs, the most
important baton exchange style is the sprint pass. This style is most
effectively used as an exchange when the incoming runner has completed a
leg of 110 yards or less, and when the relay team members have had adequate
practice *together* in the exchange technique.

The sprint pass is a blind exchange in which the receiving runner assumes that the performance of her incoming teammate is at a maximum
level, and because of this fact the successful completion of an exchange is
always somewhat of a gamble. In relays with short legs, however, the sprint
pass is practically compulsory, and with adequate practice the risks involved are not unacceptable.

In the performance of the sprint pass, the receiver takes a position at the
beginning of the 20-meter exchange zone, and in the outside half of her
lane. Placing the toe of her left shoe slightly behind and slightly to the
left of the heel of her right shoe, the runner pivots on the balls of both
feet toward the inside of the track as far as is necessary for her to view
comfortably the approach of her teammate. As the incoming girl reaches
a predetermined point in front of the exchange zone, the receiver turns
her body and attention to the front and begins a maximum effort sprint,
driving hard with both arms. After four full strides, the left arm is extended
downward and slightly to the rear, palm turned inward, with the thumb

forming a V-shaped pocket for receiving the baton (see Fig. 12a). Ideally, at this instant the incoming runner has closed on the receiver and completes the pass with an upward motion of a normal forward right arm swing (see Fig. 12b).

It should be noted that the receiver does not take the baton from the passer. In the blind exchange it is the passer's responsibility to place the baton accurately in the receiver's grasp, and for this reason the latter must provide a steady, easily seen target with her extended left hand.

As soon as the baton has been exchanged the receiver becomes the passer, and her first movement, aside from running, is to shift the baton from the left hand to the right. This transfer is of vital importance in order for the runner to be ready for the subsequent exchange, and the switch to the proper carrying hand as soon as the pass is completed should become so habitual that it is performed automatically whenever a baton is received (see Fig. 12c).

The carry is made holding the baton well toward one end. Approximately two-thirds of the baton length should project from the runner's grasp in order to provide maximum insurance that the pass will be completed once the baton has been placed in the receiver's hand.

As soon as the exchange zone is sighted at the completion of a leg, the passer should select a course aiming for a position slightly off her teammate's left shoulder—that is, toward the inside of the lane in which the exchange is to be made. Running to the side of the receiver rather than directly at her provides each of the runners with an assigned clear running path through the exchange zone. There is no excuse for relay team members jostling each other during a pass. Despite this fact, innumerable instances of self-imposed hindrances due to various types of body contact are common occurrences in most relay races. Reservation of the inside half of the lane for possible overrunning by the incoming girl can save valuable seconds in the exchange zone.

A frequently observed serious error on the part of the passer is that of running the final 10 or 15 yards of a leg with one arm rigidly extending the baton forward in preparation for making the exchange. Optimum running form cannot be maintained without coordinated, balancing arm action, and there is certainly no reason for disrupting normal form during or prior to the pass. The actual exchange should be made with an upward motion at the forward extension of a normal swing of the passer's right arm.

The responsibility of the receiver in the sprint pass is to begin her take-off exactly as the passer reaches a predetermined point which will permit the most efficient exchange. The distance between this point and the start of the exchange zone must be worked out in practice sessions between the two girls involved in each baton pass.

An effective method of determining this distance is to scratch a line on the track surface to represent the beginning of the exchange zone. From

(a) Receiving position.

(b) The exchange.

(c) Baton shift.

**Fig. 12.** The sprint pass.

55

this point the receiver paces off six strides down the track in the direction from which her teammate will approach. Here she scratches another mark on the track, and then returns to the exchange zone where she assumes the previously recommended position of readiness, and focuses her attention on the passer. The latter sprints toward the receiver from at least 40 yards out, and as she reaches the mark scratched on the track six paces from the exchange zone, the receiver begins her sprint. If she runs away from the passer, the scratch mark must be moved closer to the zone; if she is overrun, it must be moved back. Through repeated trials the optimum distance can be determined for each exchange pair on the relay team. As the two girls involved in each pass continue to practice together, they will gain in assurance, as well as in skill, and by the time of the competitive season, each receiver should be able to place a precisely measured mark that will serve as a starting signal for fast, exact, and successful exchanges between herself and a particular teammate.

### THE STANDARD PASS

The standard pass is a visual pass, and is the recommended exchange for any relay leg in which the incoming runner runs more than 110 yards. Inexperienced relay runners, or those who have not practiced blind passing techniques together, would be well advised to use the standard pass in preference of the sprint pass for all relays.

In the performance of the standard pass, the receiving runner takes a position at the beginning of the exchange zone, and in the outside half of the lane. The toe of her left shoe is placed about 3 inches behind and slightly to the left of the heel of her right shoe, and the athlete rotates on the balls of both feet approximately 45 degrees toward the *inside* of the track. From this position, which should be one of comfortable readiness, the runner reaches back with her left arm as if she were offering to shake hands, and turns the palm upward to provide a maximum target for the baton. The athlete is now in a position from which she can observe readily the condition of her teammate and other strategically important aspects of the race, yet still maintain her orientation with respect to the inner curbing and the path she plans to run. The important consideration in this regard is that the waiting runner *does not turn her back on the inside of the track* and thus does not lose the all-important visual alignment with her running course. With the commonly used procedure of passing from the left hand to the right hand, even the most experienced runners lose precious fractions of seconds in making the mental adjustment necessary in shifting their attention forward after receiving the baton.

Presupposing adequate skill on the part of both runners involved in a standard pass, the receiving runner is the one who must assume the major responsibility for its successful execution. This is a rather obvious observation, since at the exchange the incoming teammate is performing in an all-out endeavor, and should be near the limit of her endurance. In this condition she is not likely to be able to undertake any particular responsibility beyond that of maintaining her effort until the pass has been completed. The receiving athlete decides on the strategy to use, and becomes accountable for the judgments she makes.

As the incoming runner approaches, the waiting receiver determines when to begin running and how fast to run, basing her decisions upon the finishing effort of her teammate (see Fig. 13a). In the standard pass it is imperative that the receiver watch the incoming runner until the pass is completed and that she provide a clearly visible target with her extended left hand. One of the problems of the receiver at this point is to avoid running diagonally across the incoming runner's half of their lane. The receiver should time her acceleration in such a manner that the pass is made at the optimum reach of both runners (see Fig. 13b) and that she pulls away from the incoming teammate as soon as the exchange has been made. Overrunning on the part of the passer is a costly error in terms of exchange time, and the avoidance of this situation is the responsibility of the receiver alone. The incoming runner should begin her deceleration only after the baton has been passed. The receiver shifts the baton to the right hand on the first stride after the pass is completed (see Fig. 13c).

The chief concern of the receiver is to make sure that the exchange is completed and that it takes place between the zone limits. Within the framework of this responsibility, the 20 meters of the area can be advantageously used by the alert, well-coached receiver.

Normally, this girl's decisions will depend directly upon the physical condition of the runner from whom she is to receive the baton. If the incoming girl is finishing strong and fast, the receiver should time her start in such a manner that the actual exchange will take place in the second half of the zone. On the other hand, if the approaching athlete is in a weakened state, the receiver should plan her start so that the baton is passed in the front half of the exchange area. The logical principle in operation in these suggestions is that the team should always take advantage of a runner who is running well by letting her run more than her normal leg distance, and reduce the liability of the girl finishing poorly by cutting down on the distance that she runs.

In meets where many teams are entered, jamups are common occurrences in the exchange zones. A profitable stratagem in situations of this nature is for the receiver to time the exchange so that it takes place in the last part of the zone, thus avoiding to a large extent the inevitable crowding and jostling in the middle section of the area.

(a) Receiving position.

(b) The exchange.

(c) Baton shift.

**Fig. 13.** The standard pass.

58

## RUNNING ORDER

The second fastest runner is usually entered as the leadoff member of the team, but other circumstances must be considered by the coach in selecting the runner for this position. If the relay is not run in lanes, for example, the inevitable crush on the first turn is often a significant factor in the final outcome of the race. In such a situation, especially if there are many entries, it is usually wise to run the strongest, or the most experienced girl first. Another important consideration is the fact that the leadoff runner can disqualify the entire team by inadvertent false starts. Because of this responsibility, many coaches feel that the first runner should be the steadiest, most dependable girl on the team. In most sprint relay races, even with lanes, the exchange zones are congested, with all teams making their passes at approximately the same time, and it often is advantageous to get an immediate lead in order that the team will be out in front of the melee during the exchange. Even a few tenths of a second may be significant under these conditions, and strategy often calls for running the fastest girl first in order to build up this slight but important lead.

The second leg is usually assigned to the third best runner, and the third leg to the slowest girl on the team. At times this order is reversed. Some coaches place the middle two runners on the basis of the running order employed by the key opponent in a race. Such seeding of individuals is a defensive tactic often used by a coach who has a slightly superior team, but who doesn't feel secure about competing against a rearranged lineup of the opposition.

Under normal conditions, it is usually sound tactics to position the best runner last. For one thing, regardless of the vagaries of fate during the first three legs of a race, so long as the fastest girl on the team is running the anchor leg, the team is always in contention. Another important consideration is a morale factor. As long as the members of a relay team know that the top girl for the job is running the anchor leg, each will usually give her full effort to provide the final runner with the best possible position. The same psychology can work in reverse and result in subpar individual performances, when the first three girls on a team know that the anchor runner is anything less than the best choice for the position. If the other members of the team feel that the final runner cannot possibly maintain or improve any position their efforts may give her, their motivation is not likely to be high.

It is strongly recommended that the running order for the various relay events be determined as early as feasible in the preseason training and that team members put in several months of drill in making baton exchanges in the order in which they are to run. Although all members of a track squad should be familiar in a general way with the problems involved in running any position of a relay race, definite running assignments made early enough in the season to allow a great deal of practice between the most probable passing pairs will materially reduce exchange zone time.

### COMPARATIVE TYPICAL PERFORMANCES

| Relay Events | Physical Education Classes | | Competitive | | | |
|---|---|---|---|---|---|---|
| | High School | College | High School | College | National Class | International Class |
| 440 yards (402.34 m) | :64.0 | :65.0 | :53.0 | :54.0 | :49.0 | :46.0 |
| 400 meters (437 yds., 1 ft. 4 in.) | :63.5 | :64.5 | :52.5 | :53.5 | :48.7 | :45.7 |
| 880 yards (804.67 m) | 2:27.0 | 2:32.0 | 1:56.0 | 1:56.0 | 1:50.0 | 1:42.0 |
| 800 meters (874 yds., 2 ft. 8 in.) | 2:24.0 | 2:29.0 | 1:54.0 | 1:54.0 | 1:49.0 | 1:41.0 |
| 880 yards medley (220, 110, 110, and 440 yds.) | — | — | 2:03.0 | 2:03.0 | 1:53.0 | 1:44.0 |
| 800 meters medley (200, 100, 100, and 400 m) | — | — | 2:01.0 | 2:01.0 | 1:52.0 | 1:43.0 |
| Mile (1609.3 m) | — | — | 4:25.0 | 4:25.0 | 4:00.0 | 3:45.0 |
| 1600 meters (1749 yds., 2 ft. 4 in.) | — | — | 4:21.0 | 4:21.0 | 3:58.0 | 3:43.0 |

# 6

# The Character-Building
# Middle Distance
# and Distance Runs

## BACKGROUND

The first national championship meet for women was held in Austria in 1918, and a 400-meter race was one of two running events on the program. Middle distance contests were also included in the first international meet, held in Monte Carlo in 1921, where races were run over distances of 250 meters and 800 meters. During that same year, in an international meet between France and Great Britain, both a 300-meter and a 1000-meter event were contested. Obviously, women have been interested in distances other than short sprints from the earliest days of modern track and field meets, but, just as obviously, in the beginning there was little agreement upon appropriate lengths for such events. The First Women's Olympic Games, held in Paris in 1922, included the 300-meter and the 1000-meter runs, and apparently these two distances became more or less standardized events for a period of several years simply because they seemed like logical reductions of the men's long-standing standard 400 meters and 1500 meters.

In the United States, an 800-meter event was included in the National AAU Women's Championships of 1927 and 1928, and then discontinued until 1958. Marcelle Barkley was the first national champion with a time of 2:36.6.

By 1928, the 800 meters had become accepted universally as a standard event for women. The race was included in the first Olympic Games program for women at Amsterdam in 1928, where it was won by Germany's Linda Radke in the world record time of 2:16.8. After this initial contest the event was deleted from the Olympic program until 1960, but it continued to appear as a regular race in national and international meets the world over (except in the United States). Twenty-four years after Amsterdam, the continuing popularity of this distance finally pressured the IAAF Congress into approving flat races for women up to 880 yards, and recommending the reintroduction of the 800-meter race in the Olympic Games program. This event made its second appearance in the Rome Games of 1960, where Russia's Lyudmila Shevcova-Lisenko was the victor in 2:04.3.

The 400-meter run was first included as an Olympic event at Tokyo in 1964. In general, although this race (and the 440-yard distance) has not been uncommon in women's competition from the time of the earliest meets, until relatively recently it has not been as popular as the 800-meter event. In the United States the quarter-mile was not included as a standard event in national competition until 1958.

As might be expected with such recent additions to a national track and field program which has never been adequately promoted, the United States has produced few world-class athletes in the longer running races. A most satisfying exception to this truism, in terms of national pride, was the performance of the Americans at the Mexico City Olympics. Here our women were second only to the British runners in middle distance team strength. Madeline Manning's stunning victory in the 800 meters coupled with Doris Brown's fifth place in the same event, and Jarvis Scott's sixth in the 400 (only .7 of a second off the winning time), provided an unprecedented coup for U.S. girls in international distance running competition. To the uninitiated, it seemed possible that a new era was at hand. Unfortunately, however, this extraordinary cluster of world-class running performances was not the result of a planned, ongoing development program, but rather a most fortunate coincidental coming together of a few dedicated and talented people in time and space—a coincidence which cannot logically be expected to repeat itself without a significant increase in the present thinly scattered opportunities for American girls to become involved in running programs.

At the present level of world athletic competition, international-class performers in any sport can be produced only from a strong developmental program beginning with a nationwide pool in which hundreds of thousands of school children receive sound basic instruction, encouragement to strive for excellence, and opportunities to practice the learned skills in competitive experience with others of similar maturity and ability. In this regard, the track and field interest currently being sponsored cooperatively by the DGWS and the AAU has the potential of radically changing the unwarranted situation of the past. This development has tremendous implications both in terms of the general objectives of physical education, and in terms of the all-important international prestige of the United States—a significant political factor in the cold war. To most of the world's teeming millions, the outcomes of international sports competitions are just as important as the result of some scientific breakthrough, some great literary achievement, or the gaining of some national advantage through brinkmanship maneuvering.

The 1500-meter race was added to the women's Olympic program at Munich in 1972.

Olympic champions in the middle distances and the 1500-meter run to date include:

*400-Meter Run*

| 1964 | Betty Cuthbert (Australia) | :52.0 |
| 1968 | Colette Besson (France) | :52.0 |
| 1972 | Monika Zehrt (East Germany) | :51.1 |

*800-Meter Run*

| 1928 | Linda Radke (Germany) | 2:16.8 |
| 1960 | Lyudmila Shevcova-Lisenko (U.S.S.R.) | 2:04.3 |
| 1964 | Ann Packer (Great Britain) | 2:01.1 |
| 1968 | Madeline Manning (United States) | 2:00.9 |
| 1972 | Hildegard Falck (West Germany) | 1:58.6 |

*1500-Meter Run*

| 1972 | Lyudmila Bragina (U.S.S.R.) | 4:01.4 |

## NATURE OF THE EVENTS

Any race of more than 220 yards and less than 1500 meters traditionally has been considered a middle distance event. However, since it is very doubtful whether any woman can maintain an all-out sprint for more than about 100 yards, this definition is a very loose one. Conceivably, a middle distance concept for any race or relay leg over 100 meters in length might produce more efficient performance with women runners. In this regard, it is interesting to note that although United States sprinters have dominated Olympic competition in the 100-meter dash and the 400-meter relay from the first games in which women competed, they have not had comparable success in the 200. Quite possibly, with women athletes the 100 meters and the 200 meters may call for quite different types of competitors.

Simply because of the sheer physical and mental effort demanded of the middle distance runner in comparison with that required of the born sprinter or the naturally big, strong weight event competitor, the 400-meter and 800-meter races are events which tend to separate the highly dedicated athletes from those whose intent is more casual. The long, arduous period called for in the development of endurance, the prolonged and often frustrating process of learning the intricacies of strategy and tactics, and the acceptance of the necessity to keep running long after brain and body have indicated that continuation is unendurable make the middle distances the most demanding form of athletics participated in by women. And yet, for those willing to face up to such demands, tremendously worthwhile values are achievable in terms of the high level of cardiovascular fitness resulting from endurance running, in terms of the character traits that dedication to a worthy but difficult goal develops, and in terms of personal satisfaction in the knowledge that the inherent severity of these races is recognized and respected by athletes everywhere.

Women of average height and medium to slender build do better in the middle distances than do either large or overly thin athletes. Obviously, any excess weight imposes a greater work load on the body, and the big woman or the stockily built woman is unduly handicapped in these events. On the other hand, the 400 and the 800 meters demand a great amount of exhaustive work, and the necessary relatively high degree of strength calls for a good basic musculature. These are not events for delicate types!

The ability to run fast, of course, is invaluable in any track event. All outstanding quarter-milers and half-milers are fair sprinters; the champions are good ones! Most middle distance runners are women who lack the innate speed to be exceptional sprinters, but who have been able to make up for this unfortunate whimsey of nature with the determination to make good in a closely related event, the perseverance to keep at the task despite discouragements of many kinds, and the willingness to pay the price of unrelenting hard work and the sacrifice of a great many of the immediate pleasures of life for longer-range goals.

In brief, the middle distance runner should be slender but strong, fast enough to be a fair sprinter, and have the mental and emotional set that will provide the willingness to work harder than anyone else on the team.

Official AAU events for women include the 440-yard (or 400 meters) run and the 880-yard (or 800 meters) run. The girls' division also includes the 440 and the 880, as does the 12- and 13-year age-group. Age-group 10 and 11 years lists the 440, 660, and 880 yards as standard events, and the 440 and 880 are included as official races in the age-group 9 and under program.

DGWS rules do not authorize the 440-yard run for elementary school girls' competition, but include the 440 and 880 for girls in junior high school, senior high school, and in the college and open classification.

## MIDDLE DISTANCE STRIDING

The running form employed by middle distance runners is based upon the same principles that influence sprinting. The basic difference is one of intensity of effort, and the more relaxed style of the middle distance runner is known as striding.

Striding is an attempt to run more efficiently and, in so doing, to run more economically in terms of the physical effort expended. In the middle distances this is an attempt to run as fast as possible in as loose a manner as possible. Striding lacks the vigorous drive of the all-out sprint, but with top-notch middle distance runners, this form is often as fast as a sprinter's best pace. It is not unusual to find outstanding quarter-milers who run the first half of a 440 faster than their best recorded time in the 220-yard sprint race.

The development of such an ability calls for certain compromises in style and technique that will differ among individuals. When the skill is learned well, the effective middle distance stride often gives the impression that the athlete is not working hard. The overall effect is one of smoothness, and this running form is often spoken of as a "float" or a "coast."

Runners in the middle distances employ a more erect body angle than do sprinters. Body angle is a natural reaction to the speed at which a girl is running, however, and as long as she keeps the body straight, she does not have to be concerned about maintaining a "correct" lean. A forward lean of about 15 degrees is carried by the typical runner in the 400- and 800-meter events.

The optimum stride length is a natural one, and runners should avoid any attempt to change a habitual stride length into a shorter or longer pattern. The feet should be placed straight ahead, with very little lateral spread. Invariably, the foot landing is low on the ball of the foot, and the heel normally touches the ground lightly on each stride. During the leg swing, neither the heels nor the knees are lifted as high as they are in the typical sprinting action.

The arm motion should be a free swinging, pendulum-like action from the shoulders, with only the expenditure of energy necessary to maintain body balance through opposition to the leg action. The typical middle distance runner carries her arms with about the same elbow flexion as does the sprinter, but does not use the latter's forceful driving action.

Principles of mechanics indicate that the quarter-mile and half-mile events should be run at a constant pace in order to avoid the extra energy costs of variations in speed during the course of a race. In spite of physics, however, most middle distance runners have been soundly indoctrinated with the traditional opinion that the first half of any good performance must be run faster than the second half, and in actual practice, this is what happens. Whatever the psychology or physiology which makes this so in spite of Newton's First Law of Motion, at the present writing, at least, it is recommended that middle distance runners accept this concept. In competitive quarter-mile and half-mile races, time for the distance is improved only by running the first half faster than the second half.

## MIDDLE DISTANCE STRATEGY

The quarter-mile and the half-mile events are usually not run in lanes (although there is a most welcome increase in the use of lanes around the first turn), and in such events a knowledge of strategy—that is, a knowledge of effective responses to various unpredictable racing situations—is an invaluable aid to the athlete. In the typical women's 400 meter event such "know-how" may be worth from 5 to 7 yards against a runner of equal physical ability who lacks this insight, and up to 15 yards advantage under similar circumstances in the 800.

## THE KEY POINTS

From the earliest stages in the middle distance runner's training, she should be continually indoctrinated with an appreciation of the importance of the beginnings of the first and final turns. Aside from the finish line, these two marks are the primary objectives of both the 400- and 800-meter races, and each girl must understand the vital significance of arriving at each of these posts in a favorable running position. The term *favorable running position* at the entrance to the first turn may be defined, roughly, as any of the first three places. Specifically, the lead is the best position, and in the middle distance races, runners should always attempt to gain the lead by the first turn, and to maintain this advantage for the entire race if possible. The expenditure of considerable energy in this effort at the start of a quarter-mile or a half-mile race is a small investment in the light of the resulting dividends. The runner leading such a race has avoided, by this expediency, many problems. As long as she remains in front she sets the pace; she has the advantageous pole position; she cannot be boxed; she is not distracted by variations in form and stride length of her opponents; and she has less distance remaining to be run than any of her rivals. Middle distance candidates should be coached so that front running will be habitual.

If the first part of the race is not conducted in lanes, the problem of getting to the initial turn in a favorable position can be abetted by lining up the starting blocks on a tangent with the pole lane at the curve. This holds true whatever the distance from the starting line to the first turn, and becomes increasingly important in direct ratio to the shortness of the initial straightaway.

At the entrance to the final turn, a favorable running position must be defined in terms of distance behind the leader, rather than in terms of place position as at the first turn. The lead, of course, is still the most desirable station, and the concern of the other runners must be to keep the front runner from extending her lead to an incontestable advantage. Most experienced middle distance runners feel that a competitor cannot win if she allows an opponent of approximately equal ability to enter the final turn with a lead advantage of more than 3 yards. The rather evident observation in this situation is that if one girl is 3 yards in front of another at any particular stage of a race, the trailing runner has, at that instant, 3 yards farther to run than does the leader. When such a circumstance occurs with the race two-thirds completed, the handicap involved becomes obvious.

## CURVE RUNNING

Since only one runner in a field will get the lead at the first turn, each of the other competitors must make a quick decision as to her immediate plans. Normally, the field will string out in single file with all competitors taking advantage of the shorter curve distance in the pole lane. This seemingly logical choice, however, is the wisest one only if the individual runner is ahead, or less than 5 yards behind the leader. If the athlete has not been able to achieve an advantageous position at the turn, she must sacrifice some effort either by staying with the leaders through holding an outside position, or, if far back in the pack, by moving up on the outside. Actually, the sacrifice demanded in either of these procedures is popularly overrated. During such outside running, the athlete should move in closely behind the outside shoulder of the runner in the place which she wishes to maintain.

In local or district competition, moving up on the first turn usually requires less output of effort than at any other stage of the race. Novice quarter-milers and half-milers normally ease up far past their most efficient coast on the turns, and this fact should be noted by the beginner early in her training. The best sprinters will get to the turn first, but the sprint-type middle distance runner is often the one who erroneously is most strongly convinced that she must conserve her energy by slowing down in the turns. Despite the importance of running a fast first half in making a creditable time in the middle distance races, standard procedure in women's contests frequently consists of a fine battle for the pole, followed by a startling deceleration as the girls jog a casual, noncompetitive single file for the duration of the turn. Runners should not hesitate to better their position on the turn by running outside, if the pace of the front runners slows markedly.

## THE BACK STRETCH

The back straightaway of a quarter-mile race—or any straightaway of a half-mile—is the sector of the contest where running "know-how" pays its best returns. This is the phase of the match where the competitors have the best opportunity of improving their positions, and, consequently, where each runner should challenge the leaders if she has the ability to do so.

Attention has already been called to the importance of achieving a favorable position at the entrance to the turns. This observation should be underscored by the coach in connection with the final turn. Since the field is usually fairly well spread by this stage of the race, a runner has very little chance of placing unless she is up with the leaders going into the curve.

In passing another runner, the challenger must gather herself and make the entire operation as suddenly and as swiftly as possible. The element of surprise is of invaluable assistance, and a passer should never hope to go by a runner of equal or greater ability by moving slowly alongside and then forging ahead. To succeed, the challenge and pass must be a complete surprise rush. The leader, on the other hand, should attempt to maintain her tactically superior position by preventing a trailing runner from making good in her bid to pass. The problem in this case is to anticipate the challenger's drive, and to accelerate with her. Strategy for the front runner lies in keeping the opponent on the outside until she either breaks and drops back, or is forced to expend an extravagant amount of energy in making good her passing effort. Thus, the situation for a runner in either position fundamentally becomes that of outsmarting the opponent. One attempts to pass in a surprise move, while the other attempts to anticipate and meet any such challenge. The advantage in this situation rests, as always in the middle distances, with the front runner.

## THE FINAL STRETCH

Strategy on coming into the final straightaway is based upon an inflexible rule and a seeming dilemma. First, the pole lane must be held despite the athlete's natural tendency to swing wide as she comes off the turn. Many a quarter-miler has unnecessarily lost a race by the inexpedient act of swinging into the second or third lane and allowing a more experienced competitor to pass on the inside. Besides possessing the estimable quality of being the shortest path to the finish line, strict observance to pole running forces a prospective challenger into the additional effort of running around the leader in a passing bid.

The major problem facing the field as it comes off the final curve into the homestretch is that each runner must build up a lead advantage by starting her final sprint for the tape before her opponents do, and yet the start of this drive must be held off until each girl has reached a point from where she may successfully maintain her sprint for the remaining distance of the race without breaking. This dilemma resolves itself, as in many other phases of middle distance running, into an attempt to outguess the opposition. The clever lead runner, unless she is trying for record time, will maintain her normal coasting stride and momentum up to within 40 to 50 yards of the finish if she is not previously challenged. If an opponent attempts to pass, this bid must be met whenever it occurs on the straightaway or, unless it is obviously made too soon, while still on the turn. A passing bid before entering the straightaway is normally poor strategy, and the front runner of anywhere near equal ability immediately has the passer in a most disadvantageous position. With a slight increase in effort, the leader will be able to hold her opponent on the outside, thus forcing her to run extra yardage, for the remainder of the turn.

Even though no passing attempt is made by the trailing runners during the closing phases of the race, sound strategy dictates that the leader shift from her coast to a definite sprint for at least the final 40 yards. This practice conditions the girl for the all-out effort which inevitably will be called for in the stretch of later, more important races, and it also aids in providing a velocity build-up which will help insure that the athlete will run through the tape rather than perilously easing up prior to the finish.

## NATURE OF THE DISTANCE EVENTS

Races of 1500 meters and longer traditionally have been classified as distance runs, and until recently such endurance-oriented events were not generally considered suitable for women's competition. Fortunately, the validity of this dogmatic concept was not recognized by everyone, and prominent among the doubters during the 1960s was the United States' Doris Brown. Her extended string of eye-opening (and world-beating) performances in international distance races, beginning early in the promotion of longer running events for women, proved most timely and most politic. Undoubtedly, Mrs. Brown's contributions to the upgrading of the esteem in which the rest of the women's sports world held our national track effort was a significant factor in the relatively quick acceptance by the AAU and the DGWS of distance racing as a legitimate and worthwhile aspect of the American track and field program for girls and women.

Although various authorities have arbitrarily established a specific number of yards as a point which separates the middle distance from the distance races, basically there is little difference between these two categories. Mechanically, athletes run the 2½-mile cross country race, the 1500 meters, or the 880 in a similar fashion. In terms of physiological preparation, too, the same basic principles of conditioning and the same techniques of training are employed in preparing the runner for *any* race longer than a sprint.

Nevertheless, in spite of the seeming artificiality of the middle distance/distance classifications of running events from a mechanical or a physiological point-of-view, there is a mental difference which does, in fact, type the better distance runners. In order to endure the prolonged periods of considerable strain inherent in endurance events, women who are successful in these races are able to block out or diminish those physical and psychological cues which during training and competition too easily convince the "non-distance" runner that the physiological stress level to which she is exposed must be decreased.

The typical middle distance athlete is able to accept the extreme physiological demand imposed by the quarter-mile or half-mile races because of the knowledge that the hardship will be over within a minute or two. The cross country runner (or the miler), on the other hand, with an "interminable" distance to the finish line, unfortunately can't fall back on such a comforting rationalization. She knows better! And so the performer in the longer races must have the ability to achieve an automaton-like running state in which she is able to turn off the outside world. She must be what the psychologists calls a *reducer*. Psychologically, the typical distance performer is different from other runners; she can minimize the effects of various stimuli to a degree that most other runners cannot approach and so suffers less under conditions of severe stress.

The AAU lists three distance events as official for women's outdoor meets: the one mile, two-mile, and three-mile runs (and their metric equivalents—1500 meters, 3000 meters, and 5000 meters). The mile race is included as an official event in the girls' division, and in age-groups 12 and 13 years and 10 and 11 years.

The 1500-meter run (or the one mile) is an event in DGWS track meets for senior high school girls and for the college and open division.

Cross country races are authorized by both authoritative bodies. The AAU sanctions such contests at a variety of distances, but has established standardized distances for championship meets:

| | |
|---|---|
| Women's Competition (age 14 or older) | 2½ miles |
| Girl's Competition (age 14 through 17) | 2 miles |
| Age-Group (age 12 and 13) | 1½ miles |
| Age-Group (age 10 and 11) | 1¼ miles |
| Age-Group (age 6 through 9) | 1 mile |

Cross country events approved by the DGWS include:

| | |
|---|---|
| College and Open | 2 miles and 2½ miles |
| Senior High School (grades 10–12) | 1½ miles and 2 miles |
| Junior High School (grades 7–9) | 1 mile and 1½ miles |
| Elementary (grades 4–6) | 1 mile |

## DISTANCE RUNNING FORM

Since endurance is the key factor in successful distance competition, the running form used by these runners must, above all, be efficient. Most good performers in the distances run in a relaxed and seemingly effortless manner (see Fig. 14) which they have subconsciously developed in their constant effort to conserve energy. Stride length varies with different individuals, but the optimum length is a natural one. Usually the endurance runner runs with a more erect body position than is common with the previously described middle distance stride, and because of this body position, foot placement differs from styles used in faster running. Distance runners normally employ a more flat-footed landing with the touch-down actually being made low on the ball of the foot.

Arm action is a pendulum-like motion, free swinging from the shoulder joint. The arms should be held low and relaxed with the prime objective being body balance and the resulting economy of effort. Most experienced distance runners favor a lightly cupped hand position.

**Fig. 14.** Typical striding form.

## ENDURANCE TRAINING

Improvements in performance in endurance running in recent decades have been little short of phenomenal. Some of this progress has been due to advances in design of facilities and equipment; some to the eradication of long-standing psychological barriers; and some to the greater number of participants competing in distance events. The most significant cause, however, is simply that today's distance runners work harder than their predecessors did, and through such effort have achieved a higher degree of muscular strength and cardiovascular efficiency than did runners of equal (or greater!) potential in the past. The typical present-day endurance runner is more fit physically than entrants in these events have ever been before, and this superior fitness results in improved performance.

The human body becomes increasingly able to tolerate demanding physical effort through a process of adaptation to added exertion. This is the overload principle. As the organism is subjected to work loads over and above those to which it has been accustomed, it is able, assuming an acceptable stress level, to do more work subsequently.

Unfortunately, however, this concept does not operate in an arithmetical progression, and as the person in training approaches closer to maximum potential, ever greater expenditures of time and energy are required for smaller and smaller gains. Obviously there is a point of diminishing returns at which the cost may become too high to the individual in terms of the value placed on the goal. The implications of this possibility must be understood by the distance runner candidate who would be a national-class or world-class competitor today. Such a lofty aim requires personal sacrifices of many kinds. Whether this extravagant but necessary price can be justified is a philosophical question which is beyond the scope of this text. Suffice it to say that training for high-level endurance competition is no longer the rather casual procedure that it was in a less intense sports world of a few generations ago. In those programs—which certainly were more enjoyable for the participants—fall workouts were held to begin conditioning men athletes who weren't playing football and/or basketball for the following spring's track meets. Currently, for a young athlete of promising potential, "next year" is often merely a coach's check-point in a year-round training schedule which may be programmed to peak at an Olympic final as much as eight to ten years in the future! And if the typical candidate for the distance runs hopes to compete on even terms with other women who *are* undergoing such programs, throughout the world, she must submit to the same dedication of purpose.

Since conditioning for distance running is primarily aimed at increasing endurance, such training programs must be based upon large dosages of hard running spaced over an extended period of time. *Fartlek,* varied interval training distances, and over-distance work should all be employed in this procedure.

The desirability of such conditioning, at least from a physical point of view, is accepted by physiologists *if* the program does not overly stress the organism. And this concept presents a note of caution to coaches, particularly those who are working with youngsters who are still growing. Growth makes heavy demands upon the available energy supply, and the addition of further severe work stress through distance training and competition must be carefully and continually evaluated when working with young girls. In this regard, unusual weight loss and menstrual irregularities are often indicators of excessive stress levels and these parameters should be monitored regularly. In any case, careful attention should always be given to the provision of adequate recovery time after strenuous effort. Light workout days should invariably follow the necessary practice sessions of unusual demand. The coach must guard against becoming so involved with performance that she fails to see what is happening to the athlete. The welfare of the participant is what track and field for girls is all about.

### COMPARATIVE TYPICAL PERFORMANCES

| Running Events | Physical Education Classes | | Competitive | | | |
|---|---|---|---|---|---|---|
| | High School | College | High School | College | National Class | International Class |
| 440 yards (402.34 m) | 1:25.0 | 1:30.0 | 1:03.0 | 1:05.0 | :57.3 | :54.3 |

| | High School | College | High School | College | National Class | International Class |
|---|---|---|---|---|---|---|
| 400 meters (437 yds., 1 ft. 4 in.) | 1:24.5 | 1:29.5 | 1:02.5 | 1:04.5 | :57.0 | :54.0 |
| 880 yards (804.67 m) | 4:00.0 | 4:10.0 | 2:25.0 | 2:20.0 | 2:16.0 | 2:07.0 |
| 800 meters (874 yds., 2 ft. 8 in.) | 3:59.0 | 4:09.5 | 2:24.0 | 2:19.0 | 2:15.5 | 2:06.5 |
| Mile (1609.3 m) | 9:10.0 | 9:10.0 | 6:00.0 | 5:25.0 | 5:15.0 | 4:50.0 |
| 1500 meters (1640 yds., 1 ft. 3 in.) | 8:40.0 | 8:40.0 | 5:35.0 | 5:00.0 | 4:54.0 | 4:29.0 |

# 7

# Strength + Speed = Shot Putting

## BACKGROUND

According to Bresnahan and Tuttle, the shot put event has evolved from a contest steeped in antiquity in which competitors threw heavy stones for distance. As the event was slowly refined through the years, the stone assumed a blocklike form, and in Ireland and Scotland, where the modern form of the contest developed, the weight of the "stone" became established at 14 pounds—a present standard of measurement in Great Britain.[1]

In the first contests in which women competed, this event was not standardized. Some early meet reports mention the shot as weighing 5 kilograms (11 pounds), but in other contemporaneous meets, indicated performances lead one to the conclusion that the shot was often significantly lighter than today's standard 4 kilos.

The shot put has been included as an event in women's championship competition since the first national track and field meet for women, held in Austria in July of 1918. The winning effort, and, as such, the first nationally recognized shot put record, was a 22 foot 4 inch achievement made with a 5-kilogram shot. In the United States, Bertha Christophel won the first women's AAU national shot put championship in 1923 with a 30 foot 10½ inch effort.

Not only was there an early lack of preciseness concerning the weight of shots, but during the period stretching roughly between 1923 and 1929, this event was often contested as the combined distance resulting from putting with both hands. By 1928, however, a German girl, Greta Heublein, was recognized as the world record holder in the 4-kilogram, one-hand shot put with a mark of 38 feet 11 inches.

Shot putting was not added to the Olympic program until 1948, when Michelene Ostermeyer of France won the title at London with a put of 45 feet 1½ inches.

---

[1] George T. Bresnahan and W. W. Tuttle, *Track and Field Athletics* (3d ed.; St. Louis: The C. V. Mosby Company, 1950), p. 324.

The list of Olympic champions in this event to date includes:

| 1948 | Michelene Ostermeyer (France) | 45 ft. 1½ in. |
|------|-------------------------------|---------------|
| 1952 | Falina Zybina (U.S.S.R.) | 50 ft. 1½ in. |
| 1956 | Tamara Tychkevitch (U.S.S.R.) | 54 ft. 5 in. |
| 1960 | Tamara Press (U.S.S.R.) | 56 ft. 9¾ in. |
| 1964 | Tamara Press (U.S.S.R.) | 59 ft. 6¼ in. |
| 1968 | Margitta Gummel (E. Germany) | 64 ft. 4 in. |
| 1972 | Nadyezhda Chizhova (U.S.S.R.) | 69 ft. |

In general, the performance of American women in this event has been at a relatively low standard. However, despite our past scarcity of world-class shot putters (Earlene Brown is the only American to win an Olympic medal in this event through the Munich Games), the future holds the promise of better things. With the general upsurge of interest in track and field, and the inevitable increase in the numbers of athletes competing in the shot put, conditions cannot help but improve. This event is being introduced to thousands of girls each year as a challenging and beneficial sport, and if the promotional efforts of the late 60s and early 70s are continued, performances of our women in the shot put should improve rapidly during the next decade.

Many girls shy away from the shot put through a misconception that participation in this event will result in the development of bulging muscles and other physique characteristics considered masculine. It is, of course, apparent that the best shot putters are generally large, heavy-set women, but these women are shot putters because of this physical trait rather than being large as a result of the activity of shot putting. Size is a marked advantage in any so-called weight event, simply because body bulk and strength are closely associated. The heavy, muscular woman interested in athletics is attracted to this event because of the *innate* advantage that her physique gives her over smaller women athletes. The widespread concept that school and club participation in the shot put will give a girl a markedly different physique than nature has already planned is simply erroneous. Any bodily changes resulting from shot putting will be assets to a girl's figure whether she be big, small, or in-between to start with!

## NATURE OF THE EVENT

The shot put is an event in which a metal sphere is pushed with one arm in an attempt to propel it as far as possible through the air. The shot is put from within a restraining circle, with an inside diameter of 7 feet, and the athlete must begin the put from a stationary position with the shot touching or in close proximity to the chin. To be a valid put, the shot must land within a sector formed by extending the radii of the circle through the extremities of the toe board.

Shots are constructed of cast iron, bronze, brass, or any metal not softer than brass; or of a shell of such metals with a lead center. Official shots vary in weight according to the maturity of the participating athlete.

For DGWS sanctioned events:

| *Elementary* (grades 4–6) | *Junior High School* (grades 7–9) | *Senior High School* (grades 10–12) | *College and Open* |
|---|---|---|---|
| 6 lbs. | 8 lbs. | 8 lbs. | 4 kilograms |

For AAU competition:

| *Age-Group* (age 10 and 11) | *Age-Group* (age 12 and 13) | *Girls' Competition* (age 14–17) | *Women's Competition* (age 14 or older) |
|---|---|---|---|
| 6 lbs. | 6 lbs. | 8 lbs | 4 kilograms |

The uniqueness of this event is in the execution of the propelling force. The shot is put from an initial position at the shoulder with one hand in a pushing movement of the arm. Shot putting is not a throwing activity. Rules of the event prohibit the bringing of the shot behind the shoulder, thus excluding a flinging or hurling action. The putting motion is a thrust; an extension of the arm that pushes the sphere outward from the body.

Although the shot put is generally considered to be a strength event, the actual physical quality needed for successful performance is defined more precisely by the term *power*. This characteristic may be described roughly as a combination of strength and speed of muscular contraction, and the physical educator or coach should not make the mistake of overlooking the average-sized, fast girl when seeking potential shot putters. Because of the positive correlation between body size and strength, the large, heavy girl usually will be stronger than her age group peers, but the big girl with slow reaction time and slow reflex time is of little use in this event. Strength is an essential ingredient of power, but this factor is relatively ineffectual in very complex athletic performances such as shot putting, without the additional component of unusual speed of muscle contraction. The good shot putter, in other words, is both strong and fast—she has a high degree of power—but this person is not necessarily the largest girl. Glenda Etheridge, the attractive 1962 national girls' division champion, was 5 feet 4 inches tall and weighed just 120 pounds (see Fig. 15) when she placed eighth in the 1963 NAAU Women's Championship meet, competing successfully against athletes weighing as much as 110 pounds more than she!

In working with shot putters, the emphasis must continually be on *speed*. Every phase of the putting technique should be predicated upon this concept, and girls learning this event must be thoroughly indoctrinated with the understanding that the essential aim of the shot putter is to achieve

**Fig. 15.** Glenda Etheridge, 1962 National AAU girls' champion: a 40-foot, 4-kilo shot putter who weighed only 120 pounds.

optimum velocity at the instant of release. *Optimum velocity,* in this case, simply means the maximum speed which the girl is able to control with the strength, coordination, and agility that she possesses at any given stage of her training. The force which gives impetus to a shot is a product of mass and velocity, and velocity provides most of the result.

## PUTTING TECHNIQUE

Despite the apparent contradiction with established learning principles, it is desirable to introduce the beginner to this event by breaking down the extremely complex whole movement pattern into three phases: the initial stance, the shift, and the putting action. After a degree of familiarity has been achieved with each of these basic and relatively distinct skills to the point wherein the novice feels secure in her adequacy to perform the unusual motor movements involved, the coach can then effectively introduce the idea of the entire putting technique as a single coordination from initial stance to release. This latter concept, incidentally, is vital to the development of optimum velocity. As early as possible in the learning experience, the whole movement must be conceived of as constant, uninterrupted acceleration from the start of the shift until the shot has left the hand.

## THE INITIAL STANCE

The beginning position is taken with the body erect and facing directly away from the direction of the put. The weight is on the right foot, which is pointed straight ahead on a line through the center of the circle (see Fig. 17a). This foot is placed at a distance from the inner edge of the back of the circle that will allow the athlete to reach the toe board on the subsequent shift (see Fig. 16). Small shot putters take an initial stance as much as 12

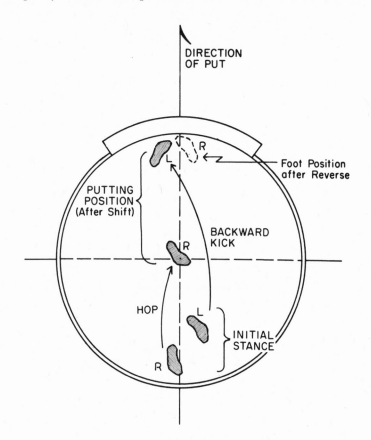

**Fig. 16.** Footwork in the shot put.

inches from the back of the ring, whereas larger women may place their foot within a fraction of an inch from the ring's inner edge. The left leg serves largely to balance the body, with only the front part of the foot touching the surface of the ground usually slightly to the left of the right foot. The position should be comfortable.

The shot is held with its weight largely supported on the base of the three middle fingers, which are slightly spread behind the shot, and with the thumb and little finger providing support on each side. The wrist is cocked back, and the shot is held in a position resting on the collar bone and against the neck, behind the jaw and below the ear. The elbow of the putting arm is pointed downward and is held close to the body in order to keep the arm under the shot. The left arm is held out from the body, elbow crooked comfortably, as an aid in maintaining balance (see Figs. 17a and 18a).

In the initial position the athlete must learn to focus her attention as completely as possible on the effort ahead. The ability to concentrate in this manner just prior to and during any all-out physical exertion is a mark of all outstanding performers, and undoubtedly it is of real advantage even to the less skillful girl or woman to be able to mobilize and channel as many emotional forces as possible immediately before the put.

Whatever the degree of the athlete's ability to achieve such concentration, the beginner should be taught that the next phase of the action, the shift, should not be started until she feels at the peak of readiness.

**THE SHIFT**

The *shift* is the movement across the circle from the initial stance to putting position. Basically, the shift is a close-to-the-ground hop on the right foot. But the effective shift is more complicated than this definition indicates, because the movement is also a controlled loss of balance backward toward the toe board.

(a) Initial position.                    (b) Beginning the shift.

**Fig. 17.** Shot put form.

(c) Release position.

**Fig. 17.**  *Continued.*

The movement is started from the erect body position of the initial stance. The trunk is bent forward at the waist, and the left leg is lifted off the ground toward the front of the circle. From this position the center of gravity of the body is moved backward toward the front of the circle by flexing the right knee, which lowers the hips (see Figs. 17b and 18b). This action places the body off balance, and as the shot putter, in effect, begins to fall backward, the left leg is kicked vigorously toward the toe board, and the movement is accelerated by a driving extension of the right leg. During this phase of the shift of body weight toward the front of the circle, the right foot acts as a rocker, and the heel is the last part of the foot to leave the ground (see Fig. 18c).

The full extension of the right leg evolves into a low, foot-dragging hop to the center of the area, which brings the leg under the body once again in order to regain balance and check the "falling" action initiated at the start of the shift (see Fig. 18d). The kick of the left leg, in the meantime, drives this foot to the toe board, slightly to the left of the center line (see Fig. 16). The left foot should touch down slightly after the right foot has made contact with the ground at the circle center.

Throughout the shift of the body to the front half of the circle, the eyes should be kept focused on a preselected spot on the ground at the back of the circle in order to maintain upper body orientation toward the *rear*.

## THE PUTTING ACTION

As previously suggested, this phase of the total putting effort should be introduced to beginners separately from the initial stance and the shift.

With the shot held as recommended in the preceding considerations, the feet are placed in a fairly wide, but comfortable, open stance—the toes of the left foot should be about on a line with the heel of the right foot, and touching the toe board. From this position the upper body is twisted to the left as far as is comfortable, and then is rotated approximately 180 degrees to the right so that the girl is facing toward the back of the circle. As the body is rotated, the athlete flexes at the waist, bending over the right leg as far as she can go and still have the leg strength necessary to drive up from this position in the putting effort. This optimum degree of flexion is easily determined by trial, and it is a factor which will increase as the student gains in strength.

The actual put is begun with an explosive drive off the right leg accompanied by a rotation of the upper body to a forward facing position. This rotation is synchronized with a straightening of the body flexion and an outward and upward push of the right arm. The body rotation is led by the right hip, and, for most effective action, the arm extension should not begin its thrust until the shoulders are about 90 degrees from the direction of the put and the hips are some 20 to 30 degrees ahead of that position (see Fig. 18e).

The shot is released at the full extension of the arm, which should correspond to the instant that the shoulders have caught up with the hip lead, and the body is facing squarely to the front (see Fig. 17c). The cocked wrist is maintained throughout the arm thrust until just prior to the release when it is vigorously straightened and followed by a forceful finger snap. The all-important timing sequence is, in order: leg, hips, shoulders, arm, and hand.

The arm normally follows through momentarily in the direction of the shot trajectory, and then breaks at the elbow as the reverse is made (see Fig. 18f).

The reverse is simply a means of maintaining balance and consists of a scissors-like step in which the weight is shifted from the left foot to the

**Fig. 18.** Shot put sequence.

**Fig. 18.** *Continued.*

right foot, blocking the forward momentum of the body after the shot is away. This technique has the purpose, of course, of attempting to keep the shot putter from fouling by stepping or falling forward out of the circle as a result of her putting effort.

## THE COORDINATED EFFORT

Although all shot putters put a great deal of time in practicing from the putting position—particularly in warming up—the novice should begin working with the total movement as soon as she has gained enough insight into the three basic phases of the effort to execute them without undue awkwardness. Psychologists tell us that the most efficient motor learning takes place when the task being perfected is practiced as a complete action and is performed at the fastest possible speed with which the learner can control the bodily movements involved.

The shot putter must strive continually to fuse the "phases" of the total putting action into a single pattern. Any pause or hesitation between the completion of the shift and the beginning of the putting effort, of course, nullifies the purpose of the shift. The constant goal of the athlete in practicing for this event should be to develop a faster, smoother, better co-ordinated *total* effort. The achievement of this objective requires long months of dedicated, repetitious drill on the complete action.

In addition to the improvement in performance that comes about through the learning process, further increases in ability will result only from an increase in strength.

The importance of strength in the concept of power has already been touched upon, but to the girl or woman who would be a champion shot putter, the increase of strength must become almost a fetish. The degree of speed of muscle contraction that anyone possesses is a hereditary factor, and, as such, is not affected by training. Strength, however, is a quality which can be improved markedly through resistance exercises based on the overload principle, and a weight training program is an essential part of any athlete's yearly work plan. Most coaches have their shot putters alternate practice days between putting and resistance exercise programs.

### COMPARATIVE TYPICAL PERFORMANCES

| Shot Putting Events | Physical Education Classes | | Competitive | | | |
|---|---|---|---|---|---|---|
| | High School | College | High School | College | National Class | International Class |
| 6-pound (2.72 kg) | 25 ft. | 30 ft. | — | — | — | — |
| 8-pound (3.63 kg) | 22 ft. | 27 ft. | 33 ft. | — | — | — |
| 4-kilo (8 lbs., 13 oz.) | — | 25 ft. 6 in. | 30 ft. | 35 ft. | 40 ft. | 50 ft. |

# 8

# Discobolos Set the Pattern

## BACKGROUND

The discus throw is an event that originated in ancient Greece at least as far back into antiquity as the Achaean culture of the Heroic Age (1300–1100 B.C.).  In the *Iliad,* Homer recounts games which set a precedent for Olympia and which included the discus throw.  The actual throwing technique used by the Greeks is debatable.  Most modern authorities assume that the throw was made from a pedestal and that the athlete was not allowed to turn or spin.  We are also told that the discus weighed about 12 pounds, and that the best throws covered 100 feet!  This would be quite a remarkable performance under the alleged restrictions.

The first women's national championship track and field meet was held in Austria in 1918, and the discus throw was one of four field events on the program.  The winning throw was 55 feet 5 inches with a 2-kilogram discus (the weight of the current official discus for men).  Babe Wolbert was the initial United States national champion, winning the title with a throw of 71 feet 9½ inches in the 1923 AAU meet.

The discus throw was not included in the pioneer international meet held at Monte Carlo in 1921, or in the First Women's Olympic Games of 1922.

In the early days of women's track meets, the throwing events were often contests in which throws made with both hands were added to arrive at a competitor's distance.  In the 1926 Second Women's World Games, at Göteborg, this was the case, as the event was won by Poland's Halinaa Konopacka with a record throw of 123 feet 8½ inches.

Women's events first appeared in the Olympic Games at Amsterdam in 1928, and throwing the discus was one of the original five contests included in the limited program.  The first Olympic champion was Konopacka, who won with a new world record of 129 feet 11⅞ inches.

Olympic champions in the discus throw include:

| 1928 | Halinaa Konopacka (Poland) | 129 ft. 11⅞ in. |
|------|------|------|
| 1932 | Lillian Copeland (United States) | 133 ft. 2 in. |
| 1936 | Gisela Mauermeyer (Germany) | 156 ft. 3³⁄₁₆ in. |
| 1948 | Michelene Ostermeyer (France) | 137 ft. 6½ in. |
| 1952 | Nina Romaschkova (U.S.S.R.) | 168 ft. 8½ in. |
| 1956 | Olga Fikotova (Czechoslovakia) | 176 ft. 1½ in. |
| 1960 | Nina Ponomaryeva (Romaschkova) (U.S.S.R.) | 180 ft. 8 in. |
| 1964 | Tamara Press (U.S.S.R.) | 187 ft. 10¾ in. |
| 1968 | Lia Manoliu (Rumania) | 191 ft. 2½ in. |
| 1972 | Faina Myelnik (U.S.S.R.) | 218 ft. 7 in. |

Aside from Earlene Brown and Olga Connolly (née Fikotova) who became a naturalized United States citizen after marriage to the 1956 Olympic hammer throw champion Harold Connolly, this country has had no other world-class discus throwers since 1932 when Lillian Copeland and Ruth Osburn finished one-two at the Los Angeles Olympics.

As with other events, however, the performance of American girls and women in the discus throw should improve tremendously over the next few years if interest in track and field continues to grow at its current rate in the public schools. Up until the present time, few American girls have ever seen a discus except from the grandstand at a boys' track meet, and only an infinitesimally small percentage of the female school-age population has had the opportunity actually to hold one—much less to receive coaching in the technique of the event!

Fortunately, this situation is being improved everywhere almost daily. This improvement will accelerate as rapidly as women physical educators qualify themselves through university major programs or in-service clinics of one kind or another, and expand school physical education programs to include track and field activities. Within a short time it is possible that literally hundreds of thousands of girls will be having first-hand experiences with the discus every school year. Obviously, from such a vast group will arise thousands of discus throwers who in turn will provide hundreds of district and area champions. Dozens of these latter girls and women will have the potential, the motivation, and the opportunity to become internationally ranked performers.

## NATURE OF THE EVENT

The discus throw is an event in which a heavy, circular plate is thrown as far as possible as a test of strength and skill, from within a restraining circle with an inside diameter of 8 feet 2½ inches. The rules of the event stipulate that the athlete must begin the throw from a stationary position, but as long as she remains within the circle until the discus has landed there are no restrictions upon her movements during the actual throw itself. To be valid, any throw must land within a sector marked by lines formed by extending radii of the circle at an angle of 60 degrees.

The discus may be constructed of wood, metal, or other suitable materials (rubber discuses are commonly used in class situations with novice throwers) and must meet certain specifications required by the official rules. The women's discus has a minimum weight of 1 kilogram (2 pounds, 3¼ ounces).

DGWS rules include the discus throw as an official event for their senior high school classification, and for college or open competition. The AAU lists this event for age-group 12 and 13 years, for girls' (14 to 17 years of age), and for women's (14 years of age or over) competition.

This throw, like the shot put, is generally considered to be a strength event, and invariably the best performers will be large, strong girls and women. Actually, however, the characteristic needed to throw any weight is power—a combination of strength and speed of muscular contraction. Often a smaller athlete will be able to compete on even terms with a larger opponent by compensating for the lesser amount of muscle mass with a higher degree of the speed factor. Strength is essential for successful discus throwing, but without the ability to concentrate the utilization of one's strength into a *sudden,* explosive application, the strong girl will never be more than just another entry in this event.

As has been mentioned repeatedly in this text, speed is an innate characteristic, and this natural potential is not one that can be developed. This does not mean, however, that athletes cannot become *faster.* Everyone has an inherited speed ceiling, but few ever achieve anywhere near this maximum potential. Skills can be improved; techniques can be increasingly polished, and such learnings refine the efficiency of any motor activity making the athlete faster—that is, pushing her closer to the speed ceiling that nature imposed upon her at conception.

Thus, as with shot putters, when working with discus throwers, the coach must constantly emphasize *speed.* The aim of the thrower must be to achieve optimum velocity at the instant of the release. The term *optimum* is used here to indicate the maximum speed which can be effectively controlled by the girl, and in this regard, the discus throw is the most difficult event in the track and field program for women. Not only does this throw require power, but the spinning technique used to build up velocity prior to the release calls for balance and agility, a fine sense of rhythm and timing, and a highly developed degree of skill in the very complex coordination of these elements into an effective total effort.

## THROWING TECHNIQUE

### SAILING THE DISCUS

Before being concerned with the difficult coordination involved in the total throwing effort, the beginning candidate for this event must learn to control the discus adequately from a standing position. This process may take a while, but it is essential that the girl become quite adept at this activity before beginning to learn the turn.

The discus is held with the hand comfortably spread over the surface of one side in such a manner that the tips of the four fingers overhang the edge. During the throwing motion the discus is held horizontal to the ground with the hand on top. It is thrown so that it sails flat, and it leaves the hand from the thumb side. The index finger has the final contact with the discus as the other three fingers peel off in turn during the release, imparting a clockwise (for a right-handed thrower) rotation to the throw.

At first the beginner will find it difficult to hold the discus with the hand-on-top placement. An effective way to overcome this inability is simply by swinging the discus with a forward and backward motion of the arm, beginning with the arm hanging downward from the shoulder and gradually raising it to shoulder height. Centrifugal force developed from the swing holds the discus in the hand by forcing it against the overlapping finger tips, and the novice gradually acquires the feel necessary to hold the discus in this rather peculiar position.

Rolling the implement for straight-line distance on the ground is a very good drill for learning to balance, control, and release the discus. Incidentally, discus rolling is such a challenging and enjoyable activity that competitive rolling of this nature often becomes a tension-relaxing, team-wide fad.

Before throwing from the standing position, the athlete places her feet in a comfortably spread, open stance, with the left shoulder pointing in the direction of the intended throw, and makes several preliminary swings in preparation for the subsequent action. In these preparatory movements, the body is twisted rhythmically from the knees, alternating left and right, and the discus is swung back and forth away from the body and horizontal to the ground. The throwing arm cuts across the torso at the extreme position of the body twist to the left, and well behind the body at the end of the right twist.

When ready to throw, the girl lowers her center of gravity during a right twist of the body by flexing the knees and bending slightly forward at the waist. The throw is started from the end point of this final preliminary swing with a forceful twisting to the left featuring a right hip lead followed by the right shoulder, which, in turn, leads the dragging right arm. As the throwing motion starts, the weight is on the right leg, and force is applied through a vigorous straightening of this leg. As the right hip comes forward, the body weight is shifted to the left leg, which is then braced to impede the rotation of the lower body. This leg block results in an acceleration of the arm action due to the whiplike effect on the dragging arm. As the arm snaps past the shoulder, the discus is released with the fingers imparting the characteristic clockwise rotation.

## THE ONE AND THREE-QUARTERS TURN

The discus throw turn is an extremely complicated coordination, and this fact has led many coaches to the practice of teaching its technique through a process of breaking the action down into distinct, separate moves. Such procedure undoubtedly makes the teaching effort seem easier, but this misconception may actually impede progress toward the whole learning involved. Since the objective of the turn is to build up optimum velocity at the release, the timing and coordination necessary for this goal are far more important than the mastery of isolated bits of technique as such. From the beginning, when working with novice girl throwers, the coach should stress the fact that the movement across the circle is a single, smoothly coordinated action from initial stance to the balanced recovery after the throw.

Many different techniques have been used successfully in the past by champion discus throwers. The recommended form, however, is the jump-turn with one and three-quarters turns (see Fig. 19).

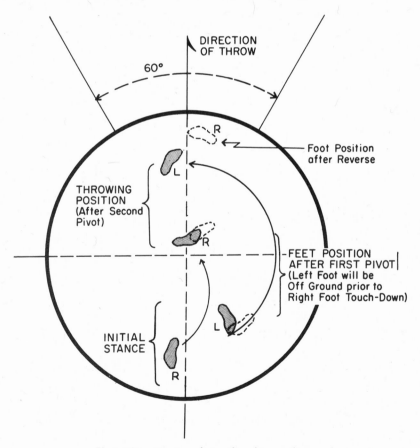

**Fig. 19.** Footwork in the discus throw.

## THE INITIAL STANCE

The starting position is in the back of the circle, facing directly away from the direction of throw (see Fig. 20a). The girl stands with her feet spread slightly more than shoulder width apart, knees flexed, and twists the body alternately right and left, swinging the discus through a horizontal arc, as far as it will go comfortably in each direction. With each change from right to left, body weight is shifted from the right leg to the left. The preliminary swings are important in establishing a rhythm pattern as well as in providing the athlete with a relaxing interval in which she can achieve optimum readiness. When the girl feels ready, usually after a habitual number of swings, she begins the turn from the extreme extension of one of the twists to the right.

## THE JUMP-TURN

The jump in this technique is from the left foot to the right, and is actually more of an extended step than a jump. The motion should be horizontal, and the right lead leg should not be lifted too high in the jumping action. The aim is to achieve horizontal momentum.

The actual turn begins as the discus arm reaches the end of the back swing to the right. From this position the body is rotated vigorously to

(a) Initial position.                           (b) Beginning the turn.

**Fig. 20.**  Discus throwing form.

(c) Release position.

**Fig. 20.**   *Continued.*

the left and weight is shifted to the left foot, which becomes the pivot and takeoff foot for the low-to-the-ground jump (see Fig. 20b). The right knee leads the turn around the left leg axis (see Fig. 21b), and the jump is made from the ball of the left foot when approximately 90 degrees of turn have been completed (see Fig. 21c). The jump is made onto the right foot, which is placed down at the circle center (see Fig. 21d). At this point the weight is on the right leg, and the body rotation continues through another pivot of approximately 180 degrees into the throwing position (see Fig. 21e).

Throughout this entire turning action, the "winding" effect must be stressed. The upper part of the body trails the lower part from the start and does not catch up until the delivery is made in the final position. The discus arm drags behind the right shoulder, and the shoulder follows the lower part of the body. Arm drag is a major key to successful discus throwing simply because this procedure extends the application of force over a longer period of time.

**Fig. 21.** Discus throw sequence.

## THE THROW

As the left foot touches down at the completion of the final pivot, the girl should be in the open stance throwing position previously described. Both feet are on the ground, the body is still twisted toward the rear of the circle but unwinding forward with optimum momentum, and the weight is largely on the right leg. The right leg drives forcefully, and the hip lead is accentuated at this point. As the hip lead comes through, weight is shifted to the left leg, blocking the momentum of the lower body, and "snapping the whip" with the throwing arm (see Fig. 20c).

The discus is released from a position slightly forward of the shoulder and at a trajectory angle of approximately 25 degrees. The arm follows through in the direction of the throw, and the forward momentum of the body is checked with a normal reverse. This shift of weight allows the turning motion to continue; the throw ends with the girl balanced on the right leg at completion of one and three-quarters turn (see Fig. 21f).

## THE COORDINATED EFFORT

The most important single phase in the unbroken pattern of the whole effort is the throwing position. The only valid purpose of the complicated movement across the circle is to place the athlete in the most favorable position possible for an effective throw. Beginners are prone to two timing errors, in particular, in relation to this position. The first of these is that of starting the actual delivery before the most efficient throwing position is reached. It is imperative that the throw be made from an open stance with both feet on the ground. The second of these two commonly found errors is that of reversing prior to the release, which results in the throw being made with the feet off the ground.

Both of these errors apparently stem from the constant emphasis on speed that must be used with all discus throwers. Velocity is of little use, however, if the girl cannot control her body while using it. The stress on speed must always be on *optimum* velocity, and this is a highly individualistic factor subject to constant change as a girl's strength and skill improve.

As with the shot put, improvement in performance will come about through two related avenues: an increase in skill and an increase in strength. The girl or woman who would be a champion in the discus throw must work diligently to increase her strength. A year-around weight training program is essential in this regard. Resistance exercises employing the overload principle are the discus thrower's best friends.

#### COMPARATIVE TYPICAL PERFORMANCES

| Event | Physical Education Classes | | Competitive | | | |
|---|---|---|---|---|---|---|
| | High School | College | High School | College | National Class | International Class |
| Discus throw | 55 ft. | 60 ft. | 95 ft. | 100 ft. | 125 ft. | 170 ft. |

# 9

# Three *Millennia* of
# Javelin Throwing

## BACKGROUND

Somewhere in the remote past, our primitive ancestors discovered that
they could survive more effectively by throwing objects of wood or stone
at animal or human adversaries, rather than limiting themselves to arms-
reach attacking or defending techniques. Over an immensely long period
of time, man gradually learned the value of the hand-sized stone in this
regard, and with this understanding came an appreciation of the ability
to throw far and accurately. Vastly later, man projected this concept, and
the stone was superseded as the ultimate weapon by a wooden shaft having
a heavy, pointed tip—an implement allowing greater accuracy and possessing more potential killing power than a blunt object such as a stone. Thus
the spear was invented, and learning to use this weapon with skill became
an important educational objective to countless generations of mankind.

With the passing of time, the throwing of the spear evolved into a
practical sporting contest, and literature as venerable as the *Odyssey* includes descriptions of such competition.

Some 400 years later, the oldest of the Panhellenic games were organized
as a regular quadrennial celebration at Olympia, and in 708 B.C. five of
the most important competitive activities of these games were grouped together as the pentathlon. The second event of this popular elimination
contest was hurling the spear for distance. The weight and length of the
spears or javelins varied, but the throwing technique apparently remained
fairly consistent throughout the 12 centuries of the ancient games. The
javelin was thrown with the aid of a leather thong, ending in a loop, which
was spirally wound around the shaft. The first two fingers were placed in
this loop, and as the javelin was released the unwinding thong added rotation and tremendous leverage to the throw.

Perhaps because spear throwing was traditionally associated with hunting and warfare, and thus with men, the javelin was not mentioned in early

publications dealing with track and field for women. No such event was included in the Austrian National Championship meet of 1918, the first track competition for women on a national level. By the 1921 Monte Carlo Games, however, a javelin throw was on the program, and the winner is recorded as having thrown an 880-gram javelin (the weight of the men's implement) 136 feet 3 inches. This winning distance represented a totaling of throws made with both hands—a common practice in the throwing events during the women's early meets.

In 1923, the initial women's national AAU meet was held, and the program included the javelin throw. Roberta Ranck was our first national champion with a mark of 59 feet 7¾ inches, apparently made with the men's javelin.

Early records in the javelin throw provide relatively meaningless comparisons with modern performances since the weight of the javelin varied, and the event sometimes was contested as a combined throw of both hands and sometimes as the best throw with one hand. By 1930, though, the event had become standardized as a one hand contest, and the weight of the women's javelin had been reduced to the present 600 grams.

The Olympic champions to date include:

| | | |
|---|---|---|
| 1932 | Mildred Didrikson (United States) | 143 ft. 4 in. |
| 1936 | Tilly Fleischer (Germany) | 148 ft. 2¾ in. |
| 1948 | Herma Bauma (Austria) | 149 ft. 6 in. |
| 1952 | Dana Zatopekova (Czechoslovakia) | 165 ft. 7 in. |
| 1956 | Inessa Janeme (U.S.S.R.) | 176 ft. 8 in. |
| 1960 | Elvira Ozolina (U.S.S.R.) | 183 ft. 8 in. |
| 1964 | Mihaela Penes (Rumania) | 198 ft. 7½ in. |
| 1968 | Angela Nemeth (Hungary) | 198 ft. ½ in. |
| 1972 | Ruth Fuchs (East Germany) | 209 ft. 7 in. |

In the history of track and field competition, American women have produced few world-class performers in this event. Since 1932, when the United States' Mildred "Babe" Didrikson threw 143 feet 4 inches in winning the gold medal at Los Angeles and two of her teammates, Nan Gindele and Gloria Russell, placed fifth and sixth, only Dorothy Dodson (fourth in 1948) and Kathy Schmidt who won the bronze medal at Munich in 1972, have been able to qualify for the final round in Olympic competition.

Fortunately, however, the present surge of interest in track and field for girls by physical educators holds great promise for improving the situation radically in a very few years. If the current interest is maintained and schools provide learning experiences and competitive opportunities in age-group track and field throwing activities, the quality of American performance will skyrocket. Up until now, girls have not been taught to throw in school physical education programs, and because of the mores of the land they have had few opportunities to learn to throw through participation in other acceptable activities. Largely because of this lack of technique, they have done almost no throwing and so have not developed the back muscles necessary for top-level performance in such events as the javelin throw. The real wonder of our present track and field program is not that we have so few world-class javelin throwers, but that we have any *at all* of that rank. This almost incredible fact is indicative of the potential athletic ability of our girls. It is exciting to imagine the performance results stemming from a nationwide school program in which hundreds of thousands of girls learn to throw properly and competitively through 10 years of progressive physical education.

## NATURE OF THE EVENT

The javelin throw is an event in which a wooden or metal spearlike implement with a cord grip is thrown with one hand in an attempt to propel it as far as possible through the air. The javelin must be held by the grip during the throwing motion, and, to be valid, a throw must land point first within a specified area. There are no restrictions upon the movements of the thrower or upon the length of run prior to the release, except that the throw must be made from behind a foul line describing an arc with a radius of 8 meters.

The women's official javelin has a minimum weight of 600 grams (1 pound, 5¼ ounces), and a length between 220 centimeters and 230 centimeters (7 feet, 2⅝ inches and 7 feet, 6½ inches). The event is an official one in AAU age-group 12 and 13 years, girls' division (14–17 years of age), and women's competition (14 years of age or over). It is also a standard event in senior high school (grades 10–12) as well as in college and open class meets held under DGWS jurisdiction.

## THROWING FUNDAMENTALS

### THE GRIP

The recommended grip (see Fig. 22) is one in which the shaft of the javelin at the rear part of the binding lies in the palm of the hand. The binding is grasped in such a way that the thumb and second finger provide most of the hold. The second finger encircles the shaft, with the end of the finger behind and tight against the binding. The first finger is extended in line with the wrist and is curled around the shaft above the second finger. The thumb is extended naturally along the binding.

### BASIC THROWING

The javelin event is a throwing activity and utilizes the same principles and muscle groups as does the throwing of any object for distance. Because

**Fig. 22.**   Recommended javelin hand hold.

of its shape, however, throwing this implement is an awkward action, and it is suggested that the girl who has done little previous throwing should learn the fundamentals of the activity with a baseball or a softball (see Chap. 10).

An effective teaching procedure is to have the beginner's first throws with the javelin consist of short thrusts aimed at a leaf, a piece of paper, or some similar target on the ground 12 to 15 feet in front of the thrower. In this procedure, the hand grasping the javelin is brought back directly over the shoulder about ear height to a point slightly behind the head. The javelin is held with the point directly on the target and is thrown forward on this tangent, with a shift of weight from the back leg to the front leg.

When the novice is able to plant the implement at this short distance without lateral movement of the javelin's tail—that is, when she is able to thrust it forward on a straight line—the target distance should be increased gradually until she is using a low trajectory and still throwing the javelin straight. At this point the girl is ready to begin actual throwing from a stand.

## THROWING FROM A STAND

As in any throwing event, the starting position is a comfortably spread, open stance with the weight on the back leg. The left shoulder points in the direction of the throw, and the body is inclined to the rear. The throwing arm should be extended straight back in line with the shoulders, and the javelin shaft should be kept in line with the intended direction of the throw. The actual throwing motion is started with a forceful drive through the back leg and a forward rotation of the right hip followed by a vigorous pull of the right shoulder. As the hip moves forward, weight is shifted to the front leg, which is braced to restrict the lower body rotation thus accelerating the forward and upward motion of the shoulder, which has been following the hip lead. The arm comes through in a straight line with the javelin directly over the shoulder. The release is above and slightly in front of the shoulder, and the javelin is thrown out and upward at a trajectory angle of about 35 degrees. The throw is completed with a straight-forward follow-through of the throwing arm, and balance is maintained by a reversal which shifts the weight to the right leg.

## THE CARRY

Different carries have been used by successful javelin throwers, but the recommended form is the over-the-shoulder carry in which the javelin is held with the hand about ear level, and with the point of the javelin either slightly above (see Fig. 23) or slightly below horizontal.

## THE APPROACH

The optimum distance for the run-up is determined by a trial-and-error method in which two teammates act as check mark spotters. Carrying the javelin, the thrower begins a run down the runway from a mark placed about 90 feet from the scratch board. Assuming that the girl is a right-handed thrower, one teammate stands about 60 feet from the starting point and marks the left foot placement as the javelin thrower runs by. At this point the athlete begins the footwork for whichever throwing style that she plans to use, and after completing the entire throwing motion, the second teammate marks the spot at which she finishes her reverse. The distance between this point and the scratch board is measured, and the starting mark and the 60-foot check mark of the approach are moved forward or backward as necessary to permit the total action without fouling. After running through this procedure several times, making whatever minor adjustments are called for, the girl measures the distances from the starting mark to the check mark and from the check mark to the scratch line, and thus establishes her approach distance. As the beginner or novice improves her throwing technique, it may be advisable to modify the origi-

**Fig. 23.**  Recommended javelin carry during run-up.

nally set distances between marks.  This is a small problem, however, once a working distance has been established.

## THROWING TECHNIQUES

### THE HOP-STEP TECHNIQUE

The hop-step form (see Fig. 24) has been spoken of as the American style because of its earlier wide use in this country.  The only advantage of the technique is that it is a rather simple coordination, and beginners usually have no difficulty in learning it.  It is a quick way to get youngsters throwing from a run.

The hop-step is executed with the approach previously established.  As the thrower proceeds down the runway and strikes the check mark with her left foot, she begins the pull-back of the javelin from the carry to the throw-

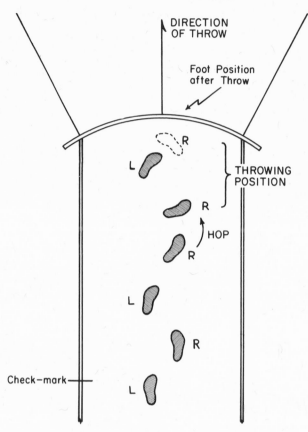

**Fig. 24.** Footwork in the hop-step throwing form.

ing position. On the following three strides the feet are placed down at a progressively increasing angle to the runway direction until the final right foot placement of this sequence is turned out about 45 degrees. During these three strides the pull-back of the javelin is completed. The fourth "stride" is a low-to-the-ground hop on the right foot, which is coordinated with a 90-degree turn of the body to the right, placing the rear leg of the athlete in the throwing position previously described. The fifth stride plants the left foot in the braced, open stance position from which the throw is made, and the sixth is the reverse of the right foot position concluding the throwing action.

## THE FRONT CROSS-OVER TECHNIQUE

The front cross-over form (see Fig. 25) is a more complicated skill than the hop-step, but the additional time and effort required to learn the tech-

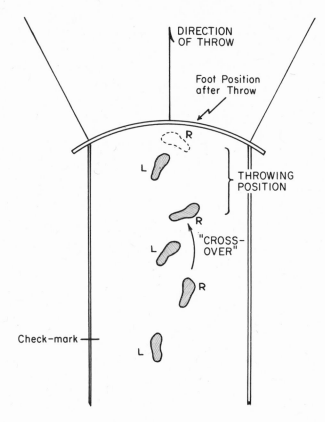

**Fig. 25.** Footwork in the front cross-over throwing form.

nique is worthwhile in terms of improved performance. Many of the world's outstanding javelin throwers use the front cross-over or some variation of this style.

The approach is executed similarly to the hop-step up to the check mark. As the left foot of the thrower strikes this point, the pull-back of the javelin begins. On the first subsequent stride (see Fig. 26a), the right foot is turned slightly outward, and this is followed by a left foot placement angled some 60 degrees to the right of the running direction, which turns the body about a quarter turn to the right. The so-called "cross-over" comes next as the right foot swings by the left leg (see Fig. 26b) and is placed down at a 90-degree angle to the running path. This is the rear leg in the throwing position, and the pull-back of the javelin is completed by this point. The fourth step is the placement of the left leg in the open stance position from which the throw is executed (see Fig. 26c), and the fifth step is the reverse to the right foot after the throw is made.

a                                                    b

**Fig. 26.** Javelin throwing form with the front crossover footwork.

c

## THE FINNISH TECHNIQUE

In an attempt to avoid the deceleration inherent in the final steps of the approach run of either the hop-step or the cross-over techniques, European throwers have evolved a style which modifies the traditional open throwing stance in which the pelvis is positioned roughly parallel to the shoulder girdle. This modification, called the Finnish style, is one in which the hips are kept squarely to the front and only the upper body is turned to the right

**Fig. 27.**    Javelin throwing position with the Finnish form. Note hip position relative to shoulder girdle position.

in preparation for the throw (see Fig. 27). Since the pelvis is not rotated, the feet can be placed down in a straight-ahead position throughout the run-up and subsequent throwing action, and since there is no cross-over maneuver to complicate the effort, it is possible to maintain whatever approach speed has been established until the throw is made.

The basic difference between the Finnish style and other standard forms is that the older techniques all involved footwork aimed at placing the body in an open stance throwing position in which both the shoulder girdle and the pelvis were parallel to the direction of the throw. In the Finnish style the pelvis and the shoulders are at right angles to each other. The upper torso and shoulders are turned to the right to a position approximately parallel to the direction of throw, but the hips remain positioned facing directly forward (see Fig. 28).

In using this technique, the thrower lands on the heel of the right foot as she prepares to make the final step in the run-up. The foot is pointed forward and the body has a definite backward lean. The shoulders are turned to the right parallel with the line of the javelin, and the throwing arm is extended to the rear—the throw must begin from as far back as possible. The throwing position is reached as the left leg comes through with the foot landing on the heel and blocking the forward momentum of the body.

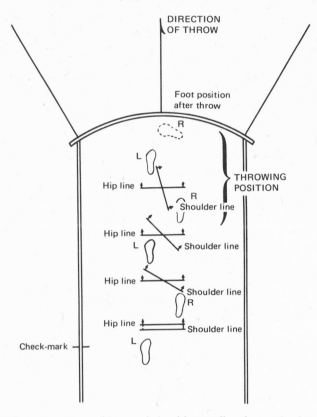

**Fig. 28.** Relative positions of hip and shoulder girdles during final strides of run-up in the Finnish throwing form.

This braking not only triggers the throw, but also accelerates the arm action due to the resulting whip-like effect.

The underlying concept of the Finnish style is simply that the more velocity which a thrower can achieve during her run-up, and the quicker she can stop at the throwing position, the more momentum she will be able to apply to the throwing effort.

## CONDITIONING

Javelin throwing is the most strenuous of all track and field events in terms of the intensity of the forces to which the body is subjected. For her own safety, the javelin thrower must work harder in conditioning herself, throughout the year, than the candidates for any other event. A carefully planned weight training program is essential, and special exercises for strengthening and toughening the natural protectors of the vulnerable elbow and shoulder joints should become a habitual part of the year-around training routine.

The extreme hazardousness of this activity due to the stresses placed on the body underscore several other vitally important precautions. First, the athlete must always warm up *adequately* prior to throwing. Despite the confusing evidence that has come from our research laboratories during recent years, a vast amount of empirical experience has accumulated indicating that the procedure of warming up seems to result in a decrease of sports injuries. Second, the girl must avoid too many all-out throws during any one practice session. Hard throwing is essential and should be a regular part of the training program throughout the year, but a few such efforts at any one time are sufficient—and even these few must follow an extended warm-up and a gradually increasing throwing effort.

### COMPARATIVE TYPICAL PERFORMANCES

| Event | Physical Education Classes | | Competitive | | | |
|---|---|---|---|---|---|---|
| | High School | College | High School | College | National Class | International Class |
| Javelin throw | — | 60 ft. | — | 120 ft. | 165 ft. | 185 ft. |

# 10

# Americans Couldn't Leave Out the Baseball Throw!

## BACKGROUND

Throwing as a technique useful in food gathering, in hunting, in self-defense, and in warfare has been so closely allied with survival throughout the million years, more or less, of evolutionary development from the maker of the first stone tool to modern man that it has been called a natural or racial movement. As with other such movements, great value became attached to skill in throwing, and from a primitive educational objective this motor activity gradually evolved into a practical sport. Shot putting, discus throwing, and javelin throwing are all ramifications of this racial need to throw, and in the United States, obviously because of the national interest in baseball, several contests involving the throwing of balls for distance have become standard track and field events.

At the present time, the baseball throw is an AAU event only in the age-group classifications. Originally it was included on the women's program, and the first national title holder was Elinor Churchill, who won the event in the initial AAU Women's Championships of 1923, with a throw of 234 feet 5¾ inches. The all-time best mark is a 296 foot throw by "Babe" Didrikson in 1931.

The basketball throw and the 12-inch softball throw are standard events in all DGWS classifications. The basketball throw for distance was formerly included in the AAU indoor program, and the American record in this event was established by Earlene Brown in winning the 1958 national title with a throw of 135 feet 2 inches.

## NATURE OF THE EVENTS

Although the sidearm throw, regrettably used by most girl basketball throwers, calls for a discus-throwing technique in order to be really effective, all of the ball-throwing events are primarily either lead-ups to, or substitutes for, the traditional javelin throw. The same principles that apply to throwing the javelin for distance apply equally as well to the ball throws, and the techniques employed in all of these events are analogous. Because of this basic similarity, and because small balls, at least, are easier to handle than the javelin, many coaches find it logical to teach throwing form and footwork techniques to youngsters through the use of a baseball or softball. Other considerations come into the picture, too. Javelin throwing is not only a difficult activity to master, but it is also a most hazardous one. Many state high school athletic federations have ruled this event out of all track and field competition under their jurisdiction as a safety precaution. The substitution of ball-throwing contests is an attempt to keep an event similar to the traditional javelin throw in the program.

Under AAU rules, the baseball throw is made from the javelin throwing area, and is measured in the same manner as is the javelin event. DGWS rules for the softball and basketball throws are similar except that a straight scratch line 10 feet long and 2 inches wide may be used in place of the standard javelin throwing area layout.

## BASEBALL AND SOFTBALL THROWING TECHNIQUE

If there is a valid reason for having a substitute for the javelin event, the baseball and softball throws are logical choices. The same mechanical principles apply and the same muscle groups are used. Except for the hand hold and the carry during the run-up, the execution of the baseball and softball throws is similar to that of the javelin.

### THE BASEBALL GRIP

The baseball grip (see Fig. 29) is one in which the ball is held firmly against the first phalanges of the first two fingers and resting on the fleshy cushion of the palm just under the fingers. The forefinger and second finger are placed over the top of the ball with the tips spread about three-quarters of an inch apart. The thumb is under the forefinger side of the ball, and the third finger is curled under the other side so that the tip is pointed toward the pad of the thumb. The little finger curls loosely in toward the palm under the ball.

**Fig. 29.** Recommended baseball grip.

## THROWING FROM A STAND

From a comfortable, open stance position, the weight is shifted to the rear leg and the body is twisted 90 degrees to the right and back as far as leg strength will permit. The throwing arm is extended downward and to the rear in a straight line as the body leans backward. The left arm is extended out in the direction of the intended throw (see Fig. 30a). The throwing action begins with a strong back leg drive and a simultaneous forward pull of the right hip that forcefully twists the body forward. This hip lead is followed by a forward and upward movement of the right shoulder and arm, and a shift of weight to the front leg, which immediately is braced to stop the lower body rotation (see Fig. 30b) and accentuate the arm acceleration. The arm comes through on a straight line over the shoulder, and the ball is released slightly ahead of the shoulder (see Fig. 30c). The throw is completed with a follow-through of the throwing arm, which then breaks across the body to the left (see Fig. 30d) to avoid possible elbow

a                                    b

c                                    d

**Fig. 30.**   Baseball overhand throwing form.

strain. A normal reverse follows if necessary to maintain balance or prevent inadvertent fouling.

## THE BASEBALL CARRY

The ball-throwing events are conducted under the same rules that apply to the javelin throw, and the use of an approach run to build up momentum prior to the release is standard practice. Check marks to standardize an athlete's approach are established as for the javelin throw.

The baseball carry during this run-up varies among different individuals. Some throwers hold the ball in front of the midpoint of the body with both hands. Others hold the ball in the throwing hand with the arm flexed at the elbow and the ball at shoulder height similar to the arm position used with the javelin carry. The simplest style, however, is to hold the ball with the throwing hand and run with a normal opposition arm swing during the approach. This is the recommended carry and should be the only form taught to beginners.

Many athletes steady the ball, as they reach the check mark during the approach run, by bringing the left arm across the body as the turn to the right is initiated, and placing the left hand over the exposed front of the ball. While the footwork of the action being used to place the body in the throwing position is being completed, the throwing arm moves back until it is extended fully to the rear at the time the right foot lands in the delivery position. The left arm, which moved across the body to cover the ball at the start of the body turn, continues with the ball until reaching the right shoulder. At this position the left hand is withdrawn from the throwing hand, and the arm is extended in the direction of the intended throw. Whatever the mechanical effect of placing the hands together momentarily during the body change footwork, the procedure seems to aid in the timing and the overall smoothness of the coordinated action just prior to the throw.

## THE DELIVERY FOOTWORK

The footwork required to get the thrower's body from a forward running position to the basic throwing stance is an extremely difficult coordination to execute effectively. The problem involved in this maneuver is to twist the body 90 degrees to the right without changing the running direction and with as little loss of momentum as possible. This rather unlikely operation is accomplished in various ways, but the styles previously recommended for the javelin throw are also recommended for the ball throws (see Chapter 9 for a consideration of the techniques of these footwork styles).

The hop-step is the simpler skill, and so perhaps is an advantageous style to use in introducing prospective ball throwers to this activity. Using the hop-step, girls will be able to throw from a run more quickly than they will by using the front cross-over.

Either the front cross-over or the Finnish style, on the other hand, are generally considered to be superior techniques, and if a girl is learning to throw the baseball for the purpose of subsequent competition in this event, she must master one of these more effective styles.

## BASKETBALL THROWING TECHNIQUE

Because of the size of this ball and the resulting difficulty of controlling it effectively during the run-up to a throw, most girls and women employ a sidearm motion in throwing the basketball for distance. This is not the best technique for such throwing, however, and it is strongly recommended that the standard overhand baseball throw be used in these events.

There is a strong suspicion that the chief reason for the popularity of the sidearm throw is simply that most participants have had no coaching in throwing a ball as large as a basketball, and that any serious practice that they may have had in this event has been extremely limited in scope and intensity.

The fact of the matter is that this throw is just not taken as seriously as the standard field events, and the typical entrant in the ball throws competes with the idea that she has nothing to lose—and may come up with a medal! Most participants attempt to throw with a form that they see someone else using, and thus the sidearm throw—a most difficult technique to tie in effectively with a run-up—is perpetrated.

As a matter of general interest, it should be noted thae Earlene Brown used the overhand form when she established the present national record for the basketball throw in 1958. Why most subsequent throwers should ignore the implications of this fact is an unanswered question.

### THE SIDEARM BASKETBALL THROW

The ball is held in the throwing hand with the fingers and thumb comfortably spread and with the entire hand in contact with the ball surface. The hand is held behind the ball, with the fingers horizontal to the ground and the thumb up. The wrist is cocked inward so that the ball rests against the inside of the throwing forearm (see Fig. 31). The opposite hand is placed against the front of the ball to steady it in place during part of the throwing action.

When an approach is used, the run should be similar to the javelin (or baseball) run-up, with the minor modifications suggested for the hand hold. However, because of the extreme difficulty of effectively changing from an approach run to a mechanically sound starting position for the sidearm throw, many competitors who use this motion throw from a stand or from a one-step approach. The actual throwing action is basically similar to that used in the discus throw.

In throwing from a stand, the feet are placed in a comfortably spread open stance, with the left shoulder pointing in the direction of the intended throw. From this position, a number of preliminary swings are made in preparation for the throwing action. These preliminary motions

**Fig. 31.**  Hand hold for the basketball sidearm throw.

consist of twisting the body rhythmically from the knees as far as it will go in each direction, with the body weight shifting from the front leg on the left swing to the back leg on the swing to the right. During this alternating right and left twisting, the throwing arm swings with the body keeping the ball on a horizontal plane slightly above the waist. The throwing arm cuts across the front of the body to the left hip at the extreme end of the left twist, and as far behind the right hip as it will go at the limit of the body twist to the right. The left hand meets the ball off the left hip before the completion of the full right arm swing and stays in contact, steadying the ball, through the return swing of the arm to the right, as far as the front of the right hip. From this position the left hand and arm delay momentarily while the throwing arm completes the swing to the right. On the return twist of the body in the opposite direction, the left arm swings freely, following the left shoulder lead, back to its waiting position off the left hip.

When the thrower is ready, she lowers her center of gravity by flexing the knees and bending slightly forward at the waist and begins the throwing effort with an explosive pull to left from the extreme back position of the final preliminary body twist. This vigorous action features a right hip lead followed by the right shoulder which, in turn, is followed by the dragging arm. At the beginning of this motion the weight is on the rear leg and the body weight is low. With the start of the turn, force is applied through a vigorous straightening of the back leg, which brings the body up out of the bent-knee, semicrouch starting position. As the right hip comes forward, the body weight shifts to the left leg, which immediately is braced to block the lower body rotation. This action accelerates the shoulder and arm motion, and the ball is released at an angle of about 30 degrees as the arm whips past the shoulder.

## THE OVERHAND BASKETBALL THROW

Basically, the overhand throw is the same technique, except for the grip, as that previously described in this chapter for the baseball and softball throws. The basketball is held with the hand behind the ball, fingers pointed up and spread comfortably (see Fig. 32), and the throw is made straight over the shoulder of the throwing arm. With this form, a mechanically effective starting position of the throwing action is much easier to achieve from a run-up than it is from the sidearm throw. Whereas the sidearm form should start from an extreme backward body twist, the overhand style begins primarily from a backward body lean.

## THE APPROACH FOR THE BASKETBALL THROW

For both throwing forms, the footwork required to get the thrower's body from the running position of the approach to the basic starting position of the throwing action is the same as the footwork technique used in the javelin throw (see Chap. 9).

Since the sidearm throw requires a more radical change in body attitude in getting from the forward run to the initial throwing position, it is suggested that girls employing this throwing form use the simpler hop-step. Those using the overhand throw are advised to work with the front crossover or the Finnish style in their approach run.

Once the thrower has decided upon her footwork technique, the length of the approach run and placement distances for the essential check marks are determined with the help of a teammate and a little trial-and-error experimentation, as previously described for the javelin throw.

From this stage of her development, the thrower has the further task

**Fig. 32.** Hand hold for the basketball overhand throw.

of increasing her skill through long months of repetitive drill on the total action, and building power through a strength training program over a period of several years. Since, to date, no one has been motivated strongly enough to pay this price, the basketball throw is the "cheapest" event in women's track and field in which to achieve success. Because of the nature of the events and because of the widespread lack of seriousness with which participants approach competition, the advisability of continuing to include large ball throwing in the program is open to considerable question.

COMPARATIVE TYPICAL PERFORMANCES

| Ball Throwing Events | Physical Education Classes | | Competitive | | | |
| --- | --- | --- | --- | --- | --- | --- |
| | High School | College | High School | College | National Class | International Class |
| Basketball throw | 40 ft. | 45 ft. | 80 ft. | 85 ft. | — | — |
| Softball throw | 75 ft. | 80 ft. | 175 ft. | 185 ft. | — | — |

# 11

# *Altius* Means High Jumping

## BACKGROUND

Jumping is one of the so-called "racial" movements of man and, along with running, is certainly one of the earliest forms of athletic contests. Just when competitive high jumping originated, however, is not clear. Bresnahan and Tuttle mention that the high jump "dates back to antiquity," [1] but there is no evidence of this event among the ancient Greeks, and it is quite evident that broad jumping and pole vaulting for distance were both firmly established as track and field events long before the high jump assumed this status.

Whatever the "antiquity" of high jumping as a competitive sport, it has been a fixture of women's contests. since the historically significant first national championship meet held in Austria in 1918, where, according to Pallett, the initial high jump championship was won with a jump of 3 feet 5 inches! [2] In the United States, the first AAU champion was Catherine Wright, who cleared 4 feet 7½ inches in winning the national title in 1923.

Track and field events for women made their first appearance in the Olympic Games at Amsterdam in 1928. One of the five events contested was the high jump, and the first champion was Canada's Ethel Catherwood, who won with a world record leap of 5 feet 3 inches.

Women who have won Olympic championships in the high jump include:

| 1928 | Ethel Catherwood (Canada) | 5 ft. 3 in. |
| 1932 | Jean Shiley (United States) | 5 ft. 5¼ in. |
| 1936 | Ibloya Csak (Hungary) | 5 ft. 3 in. |
| 1948 | Alice Coachman (United States) | 5 ft. 6⅛ in. |
| 1952 | Esther Brand (South Africa) | 5 ft. 5¾ in. |
| 1956 | Mildred McDaniel (United States) | 5 ft. 9¼ in. |
| 1960 | Iolanda Balas (Rumania) | 6 ft. ¼ in. |
| 1964 | Iolanda Balas (Rumania) | 6 ft. 2¾ in. |
| 1968 | Miloslava Rezkova (Czechoslovakia) | 5 ft. 11¾ in. |
| 1972 | Ulrike Meyfarth (West Germany) | 6 ft. 3½ in. |

[1] Bresnahan and Tuttle, *op. cit.*, p. 249.
[2] George Pallett, *Women's Athletics* (Dulwich: Normal Press, Ltd., 1955), p. 17.

High jumping was one of the events in which United States women maintained a high standard of performance in the early days of feminine competition. In the first six Olympiads after the introduction of women's events, American girls won the championship three times and failed to place in the top six on only one occasion. Our most successful year was 1932 when the U.S. jumpers finished first, second, and sixth.

In later years, a more discouraging trend appeared. Our team efforts in Olympic high jumping, to date, include:

| | | |
|---|---|---|
| Amsterdam (1928) | Mildred Wiley | Third |
| | Jean Shiley | Fourth |
| Los Angeles (1932) | Jean Shiley | First |
| | Mildred Didrikson | Second |
| | Annette Rogers | Sixth |
| Berlin (1936) | Annette Rogers | Sixth |
| London (1948) | Alice Coachman | First |
| Helsinki (1952) | | (failed to place) |
| Melbourne (1956) | Mildred McDaniel | First |
| Rome (1960) | | (failed to place) |
| Tokyo (1964) | | (failed to place) |
| Mexico City (1968) | | (failed to place) |
| Munich (1972) | | (failed to place) |

Despite the scarcity of promising newcomers from Mildred McDaniel's day through the Munich Games, the promotion of high jumping as a phase of the AAU-DGWS track and field program for girls has the potential to put a strong list of American athletes in the world-class bracket each year in the near future. The high jump is an event made to order for school physical education programs because of the basic simplicity of the necessary equipment and the built-in motivation of a self-testing activity that doesn't "hurt" as do many other track and field events. This is an event in which it is easy to interest children. Once the interest has been established, sound teaching of jumping techniques and the provision of a great deal of competition with age-group peers will inevitably result in more high jumping seasons like 1932!

## NATURE OF THE EVENT

Since the obvious effort in high jumping is to lift the body as high as possible, the characteristic of *spring* is an essential trait of the candidate for this event. Spring is highly associated with leg strength, and thus the high jumper must work to develop this factor. The taller girl, other things being equal, has a marked advantage simply because her center of gravity is higher to begin with. In a very real sense, this event is a gymnastic stunt, and thus agility, balance, rhythm, and timing are important aspects of successful high jumping. In short, the high jump is an event that calls for a high degree of all-around athletic ability. The girl who does well in sports, in general, will have the qualities to become a high jumper. If she has exceptional spring and is motivated enough to pay the price required to develop strength and to learn the intricacies of a very complex coordination, she may even become a good performer in this often spectacular event.

The running high jump is an official event in all four classfications of DGWS competition, and in women's, girls', and all age-group classes of AAU competition.

## JUMPING TECHNIQUES

Although men champion high jumpers have been using a body layout since the turn of the century, the inefficient scissors style in which the jumper cleared the bar in a sitting position was not given up by women until much more recently. Once the break with tradition had been made, however, the obvious advantages of the layout quickly brought about its complete acceptance. All but the most inexperienced present-day women high jumpers employ some form of this technique.

The recommended jumping form is the straddle roll, a jump so-called because the crossbar clearance is made with a face downward layout in which the athlete actually straddles the bar. Because beginners have a strong tendency to lean into the bar at the takeoff when learning this style, however, most coaches advocate the learning of the western roll before advancing to the straddle technique. The western roll, which gains its name

**Fig. 33.** Western roll layout at crossbar clearance.

from the fact that the style was originally developed by California jumpers, is actually a hop and features a layout in which the athlete clears the cross-bar on her side (see Fig. 33). Because of the nature of the western roll technique, it is more natural for the jumper to take off with the weight directly over the jumping foot, and for the development of this essential habit it is strongly recommended that beginners learn the western form prior to being introduced to the straddle jump.

The back layout, which has evolved since the introduction of foam rubber landing pits, is also a popular form despite its being criticized by some coaches as a style which is mechanically inefficient. This form is characterized by a back-to-the-crossbar layout in which the body traverses the bar at right angles.

### THE WESTERN ROLL

The most effective approach to the bar is one of about 45 degrees, and it is suggested that the learning jumper use eight strides in the run-up. The distance from the check mark indicating the start of the approach run to the takeoff spot is determined by a trial-and-error method similar to that used in the javelin run. Assuming that the athlete jumps from her left foot, she stands about a yard in front of the crossbar, and locates a position from which she can kick up with her right leg and miss the bar by several inches. With feet together at this position, the girl faces away from the pit and starting with her right foot runs out from the takeoff area at a 45-degree angle, with the same acceleration she would use on an actual approach to a jump. A teammate marks the spot at which her eighth stride lands. This is the check mark location and provides a starting point for an approach in which the girl does not have to be concerned about whether her takeoff foot will land at the proper takeoff placement. Minor adjustments will have to be made, of course. If a subsequent run-up places the jumper on her left foot too close to the bar, the check mark will have to be moved back the needed distance. If the eight-stride approach falls short of the takeoff mark, the check mark will have to be moved forward.

The basic problem of high jumping is to convert horizontal, running momentum into vertical, jumping momentum. Some athletes will be able to make this change effectively from a faster approach than others, but, in any case, the jumper should accelerate as rapidly and as smoothly as her ability to control the shift of the horizontal force to a vertical one will allow.

The takeoff is the key to the success of this force shift, and this phase of the total effort should receive constant attention. The final two strides of the approach are in preparation for the lifting action of the takeoff. These strides are lengthened in order to shift the body center of gravity back, and as the takeoff foot is placed down the body exhibits a definite backward lean (see Fig. 34a). As this lean increases during the last few strides, there is an accompanying lowering of the body through a flexion of the knees. The degree of this knee bend and the resulting crouch must be related to the girl's ability to spring forcefully upward out of this position on the takeoff, which is dependent, of course, upon her leg strength. It is important that the development of leg strength receive continuous emphasis during the training of the high jumper.

Since the final takeoff foot placement is ahead of the body weight, the foot is flat and the weight is on the heel. This action often results in heel bruises, and high jumpers should protect themselves from this hazard through the use of sponge rubber heel pads, or preferably, fitted plastic heel cups.

The angle of the takeoff foot in relation to the approach does not change. The foot should be placed down on a line with the run-up. As this foot strikes the ground, the outside (lead) leg swings vigorously forward and upward, and as it moves in front of the body the knee should be straightened and the motion should be accelerated as much as possible. The left arm swings forward naturally with the lead leg and should be thrown forcefully upward with the leg. During the swing of the lead leg to the horizontal position, the jumper rocks from her heel onto her toes, and the takeoff leg is straightened vigorously as the body weight moves forward to a position directly over the takeoff foot (see Fig. 34b). At this point, the body is erect and there should be no anticipatory lean of the body or the head toward the crossbar. The eyes should be focused on the bar, and the jumper should concentrate upon lifting the body straight upward before any lean or turn is initiated.

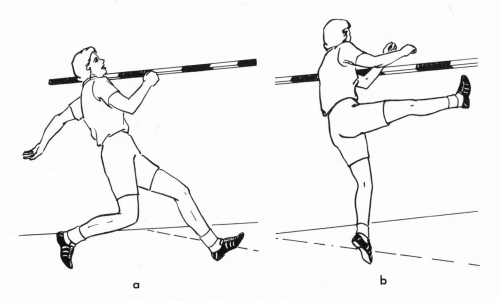

a                                                    b

**Fig. 34.** Western roll jumping sequence.

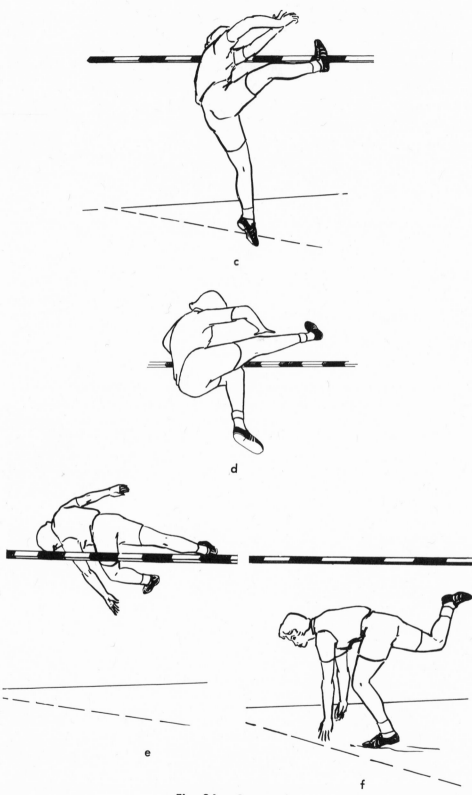

c

d

e

f

**Fig. 34.** Continued.

The jumper leaves the ground at the top of the rock-up onto the toes, and as ground contact is broken, the takeoff leg is lifted toward the extended lead leg. As it rises, the thigh and the knee are both flexed until the leg is tucked at the highest point of the jump. As the left shoulder reaches bar height during the vertical lift, the lead leg, still extended, begins a sweeping motion across the body and toward the crossbar (see Fig. 34c). This action allows the hips to continue upward to a position in which the body is horizontal, and turns the jumper onto her left side as she clears the bar (see Fig. 34d). The tucked takeoff leg passes under the body and the left arm and shoulder are dropped over the crossbar, providing a smooth continuation of the body roll to the left (see Fig. 34e). The roll is continued until the jumper is descending face downward. Throughout this rolling motion, the jumping leg continues to move under the body and leads the descent, becoming the landing leg. The landing is made on the left foot and both hands, with the knee bent to absorb the landing shock (see Fig. 34f).

### THE STRADDLE ROLL

The approach and takeoff for the straddle form (sometimes called the "belly" roll) are exactly the same as for the western jump. The athlete approaches from a 45-degree angle, using an eight-stride run-up, and takes off on the inside foot.

As with the previously described technique, the approach should be a smoothly accelerating run in which the final two strides are lengthened to move the center of gravity behind the takeoff foot. The knees are flexed during these strides in preparation for the springing action at the takeoff. The actual touch-down of the jumping foot is a heel placement (see Fig. 35a), followed by a rock-up through the ball of the foot and onto the toes as the body weight moves forward over the takeoff foot. As this foot strikes the ground, the lead leg is thrown vigorously forward and upward along with a forceful upward swing of the left arm, and as the rock-up on the jumping leg is completed, the lift-off is initiated by a powerful straightening of the leg (see Fig. 35b).

After the takeoff the lead leg swings up and over the crossbar, imparting a turning motion to the body, toward the bar (see Fig. 35c), and allowing the hips to continue rising to a position in which the body is in a horizontal layout. At the top of the jump the girl is in face-downward attitude, with the legs straddling the crossbar (see Fig. 35d). The left arm is thrown back and to the side in order to clear the bar. In this layout position, the body continues to rotate around the horizontal axis of the crossbar, and as the right shoulder starts down, the left leg is straightened to facilitate bar clearance (see Fig. 35e). With mats, shavings, or other less than desirable landing surfaces, the jumper comes down on the right arm and right leg (see Fig. 35f), rolling upon impact onto her back in order to absorb the landing

a

d

**Fig. 35.** Straddle roll jumping sequence.

shock. With more modern pits, the body rotation is continued after bar clearance and the girl lands on her back.

## THE BACK LAYOUT

For rather obvious reasons, the back layout style was infrequently used as a high jump form until the introduction of foam rubber landing cushions. This noteworthy improvement in facilities, which provided the estimable quality of a landing surface which was more shock absorbing than previously

b

c

e

f

**Fig. 35.** *Continued.*

used pit fillers, encouraged experimentation with different styles of bar clearance. One of those who developed a successful innovation was the United States' Dick Fosbury, who set a new Olympic standard with his version of the back layout in the process of winning the gold medal at Mexico City. The efficiency of this technique, from a mechanical point of view, in comparison to the straddle or the western forms is a moot question, but even the most authoritative critics find it difficult to convincingly disparage a style which was used to establish an Olympic record.

The approach for the back layout is similar to that used for the other styles described in this chapter except that the angle of the run-up is much smaller—approximately 30 degrees is recommended—and the jumper takes off from the outside foot rather than the one nearest to the bar.  Many jumpers, imitating Fosbury's original pattern, use a lengthy curved approach, but mimicry of this practice is not recommended.  With all high jumping forms, the run-up is one of the key factors in successful performance.  It is essential that the jumper arrive at a precisely fixed takeoff spot at the conclusion of each approach run, and the most effective method of achieving this goal is to establish an eight-stride, measured run-up as described earlier in the discussion of the western roll.  Any degree of precision less than perfect in placing the jumping foot on the predetermined takeoff point handicaps the jumper.  Since a long, circular approach makes this attempt more of a guess than an exact procedure, and since it doesn't provide *any* advantage, the use of such a run-up is illogical.

As in all high jump styles, the final stride of the run-up is lengthened. The takeoff foot is placed down, heel first, pointed straight ahead on the same line of the approach angle (see Fig. 36a), and the knee of the inside leg is lifted vigorously in a motion *across* the body toward the outside hip (see Fig. 36b).  As the body weight moves over the jumping foot, the jumper

a                                              b

**Fig. 36.**  Back layout jumping sequence.

initiates the takeoff by forcibly straightening this leg. The resulting upward lift must be vertical, with the body kept in an erect position throughout the initial phase of the movement. A common error in learning this style is a tendency for the jumper to throw her body backward toward the pit directly from the takeoff.

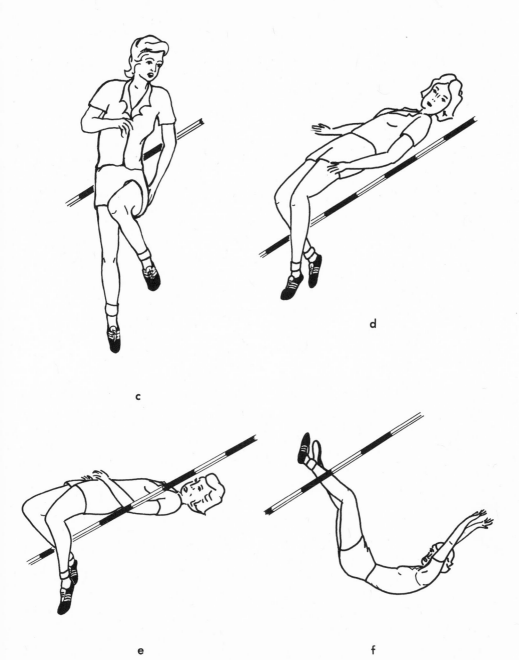

Fig. 36. *Continued.*

At the top of the jump trajectory, the entire body is turned to the outside, that is, toward the takeoff leg, placing the jumper's back toward the crossbar (see Fig. 36c). From here, as the body crosses the bar (see Fig. 36d), the shoulders are dropped, the back is arched to raise the hips (see Fig. 36e), the legs are straightened at the knees, and the landing is made in the pit on the shoulders and upper back (see Fig. 36f).

## COMPARATIVE TYPICAL PERFORMANCES

| Event | Physical Education Classes | | Competitive | | | |
| | High School | College | High School | College | National Class | International Class |
|---|---|---|---|---|---|---|
| High jump | 3 ft. 6 in. | 3 ft. 6 in. | 4 ft. 8 in. | 4 ft. 8 in. | 5 ft. 3 in. | 5 ft. 9 in. |

# 12

# Long Jumpers
# Are Sprinters Too

## BACKGROUND

In 701 B.C., the pentathlon was introduced at the Olympic Games as a grouping together of five of the most important contests. The first of these events was a long jump made from a standing start, and ancient writers tell us that some athletes jumped as far as 50 feet!

Although history has recorded no 50-foot standing long jumpers in more recent times, jumping has been contested in women's track and field from the time of the earliest organized meets of the modern era. The Austrian national championships of 1918 included the long (broad) jump, as did the First Monte Carlo Games in which Britain's first world record sprinter, Mary Lines, won with a leap of 15 feet 5 inches.

In 1923, Helen Dinnehey became the first United States AAU champion in the running long jump with a distance of 15 feet 4½ inches, and four years later at the initial AAU Indoor Women's Championships, Katherine Mearles won the national standing long jump title with 7 feet 11¾ inches.

The running long jump was added to the Women's Olympic program at the London Games in 1948. By this time "Fanny" Blankers-Koen held the world record (along with the high jump and the 80-meter hurdles) at 20 feet 6 inches. Mrs. Blankers-Koen chose to conquer events other than the jumps, and so the first Olympic victory in this newly added event was won by Olga Gyarmati of Hungary with a distance of 18 feet 8¼ inches— an Olympic record, but almost two feet short of Blankers-Koen's best effort.

Olympic champions in the long jump to date include:

| 1948 | Olga Gyarmati (Hungary) | 18 ft. 8¼ in. |
|------|------------------------|---------------|
| 1952 | Yvette Williams (New Zealand) | 20 ft. 5¾ in. |
| 1956 | Elzbieta Krzeskinska (Poland) | 20 ft. 9¾ in. |
| 1960 | Vyera Krepkina (U.S.S.R.) | 20 ft. 10¾ in. |
| 1964 | Mary Rand (Great Britain) | 22 ft. 2 in. |
| 1968 | Viorica Viscopoleanu (Rumania) | 22 ft. 4½ in. |
| 1972 | Heide Rosendahl (West Germany) | 22 ft. 3 in. |

As with most other field events, American women, in general, have not performed at a high level of competency in the long jump in recent decades. During the period between the 1948 and the 1972 Games, only Willye White has been able to place for the United States in Olympic competition. Miss White took second place honors at Melbourne with a jump of 19 feet 11¾ inches.

## NATURE OF THE EVENTS

Three physical characteristics are of major importance in successful long jumping—speed, spring, and balance. *Speed* and *spring* are basic simply because of certain natural laws of mechanics. To jump for distance effectively, the athlete must develop as much velocity as she can control at take off and, at that point, jump as high as possible in order to lift the center of gravity which will control the trajectory of the jump. The third characteristic found in top-flight long jumpers is that of *balance,* an essential need during the change from the jumping effort at takeoff to the controlled landing at the conclusion of the jump.

Generally speaking, because of the importance of the velocity factor, good sprinters will perform well as long jumpers, even with relatively poor jumping technique.

In the United States, long jumping is contested in two forms—with a running start, and from a standing position. The world-standard running jump is an official event for all classifications with both the AAU and DGWS. The standing long jump is sanctioned as an official event for all categories except the college and open classification in DGWS competition, although it is seldom programmed for any but elementary school and junior high school meets. This event is no longer included in AAU competition, and Shirley Hereford's 1958 national championship mark of 9 feet ½ inch stands as the American record.

## RUNNING LONG JUMP TECHNIQUE

### THE APPROACH

The typical jumper will normally take an approach run of from 19 to 25 strides, depending upon the distance required to develop optimum

**Fig. 37.**  Long jump form.  Note height.

velocity.  The trial-and-error technique previously described as a means of establishing a run-up for the javelin throw, the ball throws, and the high jump is used for the same purpose with the long jump.  Since the approach distance and check mark placements are more critical in the long jump than in other events using a run-up, the athlete should devote careful attention to this phase of the jump.  Her run must be accurate to within a few inches to avoid either fouling or giving away vital jumping distance.

In determining the running distance, the girl stands on the takeoff board with the feet together and runs down the runway as if she were planning to jump at the far end.  At a point about 110 feet from the takeoff board, a teammate notes the placement of the jumper's jumping foot and places a starting mark at that spot.  The jumper then runs back toward the pit from the starting mark, beginning with the same foot and running in exactly the same fashion as in the first run, and the teammate observes the landing of her jumping foot at the takeoff board. If the final stride is placed down beyond the pit-edge of the board, the starting check mark should be moved back a corresponding difference. If the takeoff foot lands short, the start should be moved forward that distance. After enough tries have been made to establish the distance so that the jumper repeatedly can hit the takeoff board accurately with her jumping foot, the distance from the edge of the takeoff board to the starting mark is measured and recorded. A second check mark is then located and measured in the same manner, seven strides from the start. This latter mark serves merely as a warning to the jumper if she is off stride, and is placed where it is in order that she will be able to abort her approach, if necessary, before she has expended undue energy, and at a point that will permit her to ease up gradually without risk of wasting a trial by inadvertently running across the scratch line.

These check mark distances will vary under different conditions, of course, but the minor adjustments necessary to correct one's approach run can be easily made once the basic measurements have been established.

The approach run during a jump should begin like a sprint. The objective of the run-up is to develop optimum velocity—that is, as much speed as the athlete can effectively control—at the takeoff board. The final three strides are often called a "coast," but this phase of the run is merely a relaxing of the all-out sprinting effort without any appreciable slackening of speed. The jumper must not lose momentum at this point.

a                                          b

**Fig. 38.**  Long jump sequence.

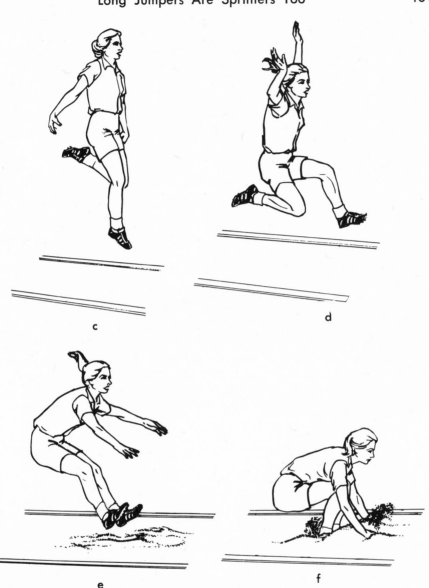

**Fig. 38.** *Continued.*

## THE TAKEOFF

The final stride is shortened about 6 inches in order to move the center of gravity slightly forward, and the takeoff foot hits the board flat-footed and with a forceful stamp. This foot placement is accompanied by a bending of the knee, which lowers the body just prior to the jumping action. The jumping leg straightens vigorously immediately after the foot stamp (see Fig. 38a), and as the body moves forward, the foot rocks up onto the toes. The takeoff should occur when the center of gravity is forward of the takeoff foot about 12 inches.

In achieving the flat-footed stamp, the takeoff foot is necessarily placed down heel first. This procedure often leads to painful bruises, and all long jumpers should protect the heel of the jumping foot with a fitted plastic heel cup.

## THE FLIGHT

Since the most important action at takeoff is to get the body as high as possible to take full advantage of the speed built up during the approach, a vigorous upward lift of the arms and the thigh of the lead leg should be coordinated with the extension of the takeoff leg (see Fig. 38b). It is essential that the head and shoulders be lifted upward; the athlete should always concentrate upon getting height with the upper part of her body.

Most jumpers use a "walking" action while in the air during the flight of the jump (see Fig. 37). Mechanically, of course, such movements have no effect upon the distance achieved. These actions do, however, help to keep the jumper balanced and relaxed, and the so-called *hitch-kick* form is recommended. The first stride of this technique develops from the forceful forward and upward swing of the lead leg at takeoff. After leaving the ground, the jumping leg moves forward, passing the lead leg as it now swings back (see Fig. 38d). The hitch-kick action is completed when the lead leg moves forward for the second time, to a position in which it is extended even with the takeoff leg and both are in the landing position (see Fig. 38e).

## THE LANDING

The actual landing is made with the feet 6 to 8 inches apart and extended well out in front of the body. As the heels touch down, the shoulders and the head are thrust forward and the knees relax to allow the jumper's momentum to pull her directly ahead (see Fig. 38f).

## STANDING LONG JUMP TECHNIQUE

In executing the standing long jump, the competitor stands with the feet slightly spread and with the toes of both feet a fraction of an inch behind the scratch line.

From this position the jumper initiates a rocking motion by extending both arms forward to shoulder height and then swinging them downward and back to a point behind the hips. As the arms swing backward, the knees are flexed and the center of gravity is lowered. From the back position the arms swing forward once again and the knees extend to the beginning stance. This rocking motion is a preliminary movement that serves the same purpose as the preliminary swings of the discus thrower: it establishes a rhythmic pattern for the entire jumping action, it allows the jumper to achieve an optimum condition of readiness, and it places her in the most favorable starting position for the effort of the jump itself. This rocking motion may be continued for as long as the jumper wishes as long as the feet are kept in place. Neither foot may be lifted nor moved as a preliminary action to the actual jumping effort.

When the girl feels ready, the action begins as the arms reach the top limit of one of the preliminary forward swings. From this point the backward swing is accentuated, the knees flex to a 90-degree angle, and the girl leans forward from the waist assuming a crouched attitude. As the arms reach the extreme back position, they are swung vigorously forward, and as they pass the hips and start upward, an explosive extension of the legs is coordinated with the arm action to propel the body forward at an initial trajectory angle of about 20 degrees.

During the flight of the jump, the upward position of the arms and the forward inclination of the upper body are maintained, and the legs are brought forward together and extended in front of the body. The feet touch down together, and as the landing is made, a forward thrust of the head and shoulders and a strenuous back swing of the arms are combined to keep the center of gravity moving forward. This action plus a relaxation of the knees normally allows the jumper to land without loss of balance.

### COMPARATIVE TYPICAL PERFORMANCES

| Long Jumping Events | Physical Education Classes | | Competitive | | | |
| --- | --- | --- | --- | --- | --- | --- |
| | High School | College | High School | College | National Class | International Class |
| Running long jump | 11 ft. 6 in. | 11 ft. 6 in. | 16 ft. | 16 ft. | 18 ft. 4 in. | 20 ft. 6 in. |
| Standing long jump | 6 ft. | 5 ft. 8 in. | 8 ft. | — | — | — |

# 13

# Staging the Show

Anyone can stage a successful track and field meet. Experience is an asset but not a prerequisite in the same sense as are interest, desire, and willingness to work.

The size of the meet may range from intraclass competition involving only a few students to an Olympiad involving thousands of officials and participants. There are also numerous types of meets—a track and field contest may be face-to-face or a postal one; it may be a relay meet or one with the conventional order of events; it may be an invitational meet or an all-comers contest; team points may be based on place scoring or upon only the winning performances. Obviously, covering every aspect of planning and conducting specific types of meets is not feasible in this chapter; however, regardless of the type or range, thorough organization is always a must. If a meet is based upon sound organization, it will be a successful experience for participants, officials, and spectators, and the suggestions given in this chapter are applicable to any situation. Details dependent upon facilities, purpose, and personnel may differ slightly for each meet director, and it is up to her to determine the scope and type of her own promotion, and then limit her meet in the ways she thinks necessary.

## PRE-MEET PLANNING

Planning should begin when the thought of conducting a meet is first conceived. The scope of the meet will help to determine the number of people to be involved. Small meets are usually organized by the coach alone whereas the larger meets are organized by a meet committee with the coach serving as the director. The meet director is the key coordinator of the total event, with the committee giving assistance in specialized areas of planning and promotion.

The meet committee should be selected carefully, making it a total school involvement if at all possible. The director should assemble the group on the basis of what is needed plus such vital considerations as to whether members are capable, interested, and willing to work. The committee should not be so large that it is cumbersome, but such a group might logically include the chairman of the physical education department, the athletic director, the boys' track and field coach, representatives of student organizations, former track and field athletes in the community, a parent, a businessman, and faculty members of the art, journalism, and business departments. The meet director should not be surprised or discouraged if she has to assume roles hopefully delegated to various committee members. The search for interested and talented individuals to whom specific tasks can be assigned should be a continuing process from year to year.

## SETTING THE DATE

Possible dates for meets should be considered in regard to the availability of facilities, and conflicts with school, community, or area events. When the date is established, preferably a year in advance for important and/or large meets, it should be confirmed in writing and placed on the school calendar. Key people—including those in the local area who are interested in track and field, coaches of track and field teams, and those who previously have conducted track and field meets—should be notified. Too, if the meet is to be sanctioned by the AAU, DGWS, or the state high school activities association, the specific association should be contacted immediately. If the meet is sanctioned, it is possible to receive additional publicity, more teams may be interested in entering, the date is more likely to be protected from conflicting events, and help may be forthcoming in conducting the event.

## SCOPE OF THE MEET

Time, facilities, purpose, and the experience of the participants to be involved will determine the list of events and the number of participants to be accommodated. If it is an intraclass or an intramural meet, the teacher has the prerogative of including whatever events she thinks will be appropriate and in whatever order seems most convenient. However, if the contest is sanctioned by the AAU, DGWS, or by a state high school activities association, the events, order of events, number of events, number of events in which a girl may participate, and the various age division contests which may be included are already established by rule.

One should not let existing facilities, lack of official equipment, or limited experience be excuses for procrastinating on conducting a meet. The longest distance run does not have to be a mile or the shortest a 50-yard dash. In informal meets, course distances may be arbitrarily established.

A 25-yard dash could be run to determine the fastest starter, or a walking event could be held between points irrespective of the distance. Track events in which the winner is the one who most nearly approaches a previously estimated time in covering the distance are becoming increasingly popular. An official track is not necessary—races may be run on a turfed area involving no curves. As a matter of fact, a grassy area may be a safer running surface for inexperienced hurdlers. Shuttle relays may be run rather than pursuit relays. The javelin and discus events may be replaced with softball, baseball, basketball, and/or soccerball throws. If there is no jumping pit available for the running long jump, the standing event may be substituted. The director should always be creative and innovative.

The order of events in any but informal meets is established by rules. The time schedule, however, is more flexible, and is usually programmed on the basis of the available facilities, the experience of the officials and participants, and the common sense of the director. Field events usually begin thirty minutes before the first track event, and the high jump ordinarily requires the longest amount of time to complete. A hurdles event should be scheduled first on the track agenda in order that the hurdles can be placed in position ahead of time. Information concerning rules applying to events, scheduling, and age division variations is available in the current AAU *Track and Field Handbook,* the DGWS *Track and Field Guide,* or from the appropriate state high school activities association.

### FINANCING

A successful meet of a wide scope cannot be staged without money. The degree of need for financial support will depend upon such factors as the status of the facilities (free or rented), officials (volunteer or paid), equipment (have on hand, may borrow, or must buy), expenses of participants (travel on their own, or the expenses paid for the "names"), and awards (homemade, medals, or more expensive trophies). Included in the budget must be such items as the cost of phone calls, secretarial help, stationery, postage, and the preparation of facilities. A track meet can be an expensive operation in terms of both energy and money, or it can cost nothing but the time of the people who do the job.

Where does one get the needed financial assistance? It is most desirable, of course, if such aid is a part of the total school budget and is appropriated as for any educational endeavor of the institution. However, this is not the ordinary procedure and, in such cases, funds must be mustered in other ways. Gate receipts are not always dependable sources of revenue and if this is the only means of raising operating capital, it would be wise to have advance ticket sales. Private business firms are often asked to sponsor selected events and underwrite the cost of the awards involved, community organizations may subsidize the entire meet, or money may be made by selling advertisement space in a program. The track and field team members may have to conduct fund raising projects to support their interest—commonly found means include bake sales, car washes, work days, doughnut sales in the morning or sandwich sales at noon, concession stands at athletic or other campus events, and king or queen contests. Under no circumstances should track and field meets be financed from personal funds of the teacher or coach.

## OFFICIALS

Officials must be contacted in regard to time, place, and duties well in advance (as soon as the date is set) of a meet in order that they can make necessary personal plans. In selecting officials, the director should be an equal opportunity employer—she should not be concerned with sex or age but only with the individuals' abilities and willingness.

The coach of the boys' team will often have a list of competent local or regional officials, or possibly such a roster may be obtained from the state AAU, DGWS, or high school activities association offices. Colleagues who have conducted meets—intraclass, intramural, or interschool—may be contacted for suggestions regarding officials. Often help may be secured from a nearby college or university if there is a physical education majors' program there. If there is no such group, there might be students who would be happy to assist in order to gain managerial experience, or even as a service project. Parents of participants are usually delighted to help, as are other members of the community who have had prior sports experience—ex-athletes, fans, or those who have previously officiated in other athletic events such as swimming meets. Students can serve capably in many capacities. A place should be made for everyone who wants to assist.

Approximately two weeks before the scheduled date of the meet, a reminder notice of the date, place, duties, current rules involving the event, and when and where to check in should be sent to all officials. It should never be accepted as a fact that all of those previously contacted will remember to appear and know exactly what to do. Printed instruction sheets for officials are helpful as are personal contacts between the director and each official. Incidental ground rules such as whether a girl may run barefooted or must wear shoes should be included in these instructions. If inexperienced officials are involved, an officiating clinic must be provided prior to the meet. Even with more knowledgeable officials, conducting a pre-meet meeting is a wise move. If finances permit, this meeting might well be combined with a social function—a luncheon, a tea, or a dinner.

Aside from the meet director, the key officiating jobs, in order of importance, are the announcer, the clerk of the course, and the starter. The announcer "runs" the show and should be the most experienced official available. She must be able to adjust, adapt, and revise calls and announcements to meet any and all situations arising at a meet. She must visualize the over-all pattern in order to maintain preliminary and final calls in proper and efficient sequence. She must be familiar with records and comparison marks in order to keep the all-important spectators aware of and interested in pertinent incidents taking place. It helps if she has a pleasant-to-listen-to voice and a sense of humor.

The clerk of the course is responsible for getting each competitor in the proper heat, in her assigned lane, at the correct starting mark, at the proper time. Hers is a very difficult job if there is a large number of contestants, and it becomes even more difficult if the participants are inexperienced. She needs to be patient but firm, have a pleasing personality, and have immediate organizational ability.

The starter, who begins all races, must not only be a capable and experienced official but must also be able to establish good rapport with the runners. She must keep the meet on schedule while placing the nervous, frightened girl at ease. Only the experienced official can give each contestant her rightful equal chance at the beginning of a race. The experienced starter is often given the additional responsibility of serving as meet referee.

Possibly next in line of importance are the scorer, chief finish judge, and chief timekeeper. For other officials, less experienced people can be used. Unless record performances are expected, almost any normally reacting person, with proper briefing, should be capable of doing a satisfactory job—especially in a dual interschool meet or one of lesser scope. Two rather important considerations are: (1) to have *enough* officials for each event, and (2) to limit the work assigned to each of these to *no more than one* field event. Overworking volunteers is a certain way to make it increasingly difficult to obtain officials for future meets. Twenty officials are usually enough for a dual meet, plus fifteen more if several teams are entered. The least number necessary in any meet will depend largely upon the scope of the meet. It is always a good idea to have stand-bys for missing or late-arriving officials.

Specific duties of officials are given in current AAU and DGWS track and field guides. The following is a basic check list of the officials needed for a meet involving many participants—a state-wide meet, a conference meet, or an invitational meet:

> 1 Refereee
> 1 Announcer
> 2 Clerks of the course (including the chief clerk)
> 1 Starter
> 1 Recall starter
> 7 Finish judges for three places (chief judge and 2 assistants for each place)
> 7 Timers for three places (chief timer and 2 assistants for each place)
> 5 Inspectors (including the chief inspector)
> 17 Field judges (including the chief judge for each event)
> > 2 High jump judges
> > 3 Running long jump judges
> > 3 Standing long jump judges

    3 Shot put judges
    3 Discus judges
    3 Javelin, softball, or basketball throw judges
6 Marshals (for spectator control)
1 Scorer
1 Typist
1 First aider (doctor)
1 Surveyor
1 Inspector of implements
1 Custodian of awards
1 Wind gauge clerk
1 Hurdle chief with helpers (at least 1 helper for each flight of hurdles)
1 Holder of finish line

## PUBLICITY AND PROMOTION

Publicity angles should be sought to promote any home meet. The school art and journalism departments may give invaluable assistance in this area. At school, a display of photographs and related interesting articles on bulletin boards is effective. The school paper should, of course, be widely used. A school assembly will give the meet director a chance to discuss the event with the student body and provide the opportunity for members of the track and field squad to be introduced. The community newspaper can aid in promoting spectator interest by publishing photographs and providing information on performances of outstanding athletes—especially if local performers are involved. The sports editor of papers that are published in other cities but distributed locally should be contacted. Meet directors often promote activities by speaking before various civic groups and by making arrangements for spot announcements on local radio stations. One should not hesitate to request publicity—most local groups are only too happy to lend a helping hand.

Promotion should be directed ahead to the meet itself. Arrangements should be made for representatives from local newspapers, radio, and television stations to attend the contest. News media representatives should be notified of the times of events, especially those contests which are expected to be of particular interest.

## MEET INFORMATION AND ENTRY FORMS

Notification of the time and place of a meet should be sent out several months prior to the date of the event (see Fig. 39). Six to eight weeks before the meet, an information packet should be sent to potential entries. Included in this should be a list of events, time schedule, equipment information (e.g., restriction concerning type of shoe, composition of track and approaches, weight of shot, height of hurdles, and available equipment), eligibility requirements, eating arrangements, overnight accommodations, special activities, dressing facilities, and entry fees. Such notification should include an official entry blank (see Fig. 40) with the entry deadline distinctly

### GIRLS' TRACK AND FIELD MEET
#### Oklahoma State University

Annual Meet                                           Lewis Field (Football Stadium)
April 24, 19—                                         Billie J Jones, Director

This meet has been approved by the Oklahoma High School Activities Association. It is being held in conjunction with the College Women's Track and Field Meet.

Eligibility:  Rules of the OHSAA will apply to all participants. You must send an eligibility list. All girls who are members of grades nine through twelve are eligible to participate.

Entry Fees: 50¢ per girl regardless of the number of events entered.

Awards:  Medals will be awarded to the winners of the first three places in all events. Championship trophies will be awarded to the first, second, and third place teams with points being awarded to the first five places in each event.

Lunch:  There will be a 45 minute break between the preliminary and final events. The Physical Education Majors Club will sell sandwiches and cokes and there are several drive-ins within two blocks of the track.

Motels:  To make arrangements for staying overnight, contact the Holiday Inn, El Sol Motel, Circle D Motel, Highway 51 Motel, or the Oklahoma State University Union Club.

Track:  The track has a cinder surface and either short or long spikes or tennis shoes may be worn. No barefoot running will be permitted. The long jump and high jump approaches have a composition surface and only short spikes are allowed, or a contestant may wear tennis shoes or no shoes.

Events:  The following schedule is subject to change depending upon the number of participants. The meet will begin at 9:00 A.M. regardless of the schedule of events or the weather. Additional information will be sent to entrants after April 19.

#### FIELD EVENTS
9:00 A.M.  High Jump
9:00 A.M.  Softball Throw
10:00 A.M.  Shot Put
10:00 A.M.  Running Long Jump
11:30 A.M.  Standing Long Jump
12:00 noon  Discus

| **TRACK EVENTS** Trials | | **TRACK EVENTS** Finals | |
|---|---|---|---|
| 9:00 A.M. | 50-yard Low Hurdles | 12:00 noon | 50-yard Low Hurdles |
| 9:40 A.M. | 440-yard Run (Finals) | 1:00 P.M. | 880-yard Run |
| 10:20 A.M. | 220-yard Dash | 1:20 P.M. | 220-yard Dash |
| 11:00 A.M. | 100-yard Dash | 1.40 P.M. | 100-yard Dash |
| | | 2:00 P.M. | 440-yard Relay |

**Fig. 39.** Typical track meet information sheet.

GIRLS' TRACK AND FIELD MEET
Oklahoma State University

*Please return this entry blank by April 19, 19—,* to Miss Billie J Jones, Director of the Meet, Colvin Physical Education Center, Oklahoma State University, Stillwater, Oklahoma, 74074. The phone number is 405-372-6211, ext. 6351 or 405-372-4240. Substitutions may be made on the day of the meet but no additional entries may be made. List possible substitutes on the back of this entry form.

A participant may enter a maximum of three events—track and/or field plus the relay. Each school is limited to two entries in each event (one relay team). After each entry, list the best time or distance in the specific event.

1. High Jump. Finals 9:00 A.M. (Beginning height will be 3'8")

    1._____     2. _____
2. Softball Throw. Finals 9:00 A.M. (12" official inside seam)

    1._____     2. _____
3. Shot Put. Finals 10:00 A.M. (8-pound)

    1._____     2. _____
4. Running Long Jump. Finals 10:00 A.M.

    1._____     2. _____
5. Standing Long Jump. Finals 11:30 A.M. (Beat board will be used)

    1._____     2. _____
6. Discus. Finals 12:00 noon

    1._____     2. _____
7. 50-yard Low Hurdles. Trials 9:00 A.M. Finals 12:00 noon (30" height)

    1._____     2. _____
8. 440-yard Run. Finals 9:40 A.M.

    1._____     2. _____
9. 880-yard Run. Finals 1:00 P.M.

    1._____     2. _____
10. 220-yard Dash. Trials 10:20 A.M. Finals 1:20 P.M.

    1._____     2. _____
11. 100-yard Dash. Trials 11:00 A.M. Finals 1:40 P.M.

    1._____     2. _____
12. 440-yard Relay. Finals 2:00 P.M.

    1._____     3. _____

    2._____     4. _____

**Fig. 40.** Typical track meet entry form.

marked, underlined, or printed in large letters. The entry date should be at least five days before the meet in order to allow time to set heats and flights, and to finalize the time schedule.

Heat and flight sheets require a great deal of time to prepare, and should be started as soon as entries begin to arrive. A master list of all contestants entered in each event must be made, recording each girl's name, school, and best time or distance in her event. The number of heats and flights neces-sary will depend upon the number entries and the size of the track. Entries should be placed according to their previously achieved best times and dis-tances—the best are scattered throughout the heats and flight. If previous marks are not available, the meet director may place the entries at her discretion, but should avoid placing entries from the same school in the same group.

## AWARDS

The selection of awards will be controlled by the budget, purpose of the meet, number of teams entered, number of places to be awarded, and the philosophy of the meet director. For interclass and intramural competition awards may be no less than home-made ribbons or plaques. In dual or triangular meets, it is not common practice to present awards, but in confer-ence meets or those involving a large number of teams, awards are normally made. Decisions concerning the type of prizes (ribbons, medals, or trophies), number of places to be awarded, and the nature of team awards, should be made months in advance. To guarantee arival, such prizes must be ordered at least six weeks before the scheduled date of the meet. In purchasing awards, one should shop around to get the most for the money, but only reputable firms should be contacted. A delivery date of at least two weeks before the awards are needed should be specified. It is often possible to save money if an order is combined with other orders for awards placed by the school.

Decisions should also be made at this time as to how the awards will be presented—when and by whom. An awards ceremony can be an impressive aspect of a meet and should be carefully planned. The most important thing, however, is to have the awards on hand for the winners. Not only will the athletes be disappointed if prizes won are not immediately avail-able, but it isn't a simple task to mail a large number of awards at a later date.

## FACILITIES AND EQUIPMENT

The meet director is responsible for checking facilities to see that every-thing is ready. If no one is specifically assigned to maintaining and prepar-ing the track area, she will have to be responsible for dragging, brushing, lining, and marking the areas, using help solicited from whatever friends and relations are available. An up-to-date rulebook must be used to determine the correct markings for the various events. If one is not available advice should be solicited from the boys' track coach. If the responsibility of preparing the facilities is delegated, the meet director must double-check the finished work. Even experienced personnel can make a mistake or forget an essential marking. Permanent markings, such as those placed on the curb of the track to indicate starting and finish lines, relay zones, and hurdle locations, alleviate the task of measuring and should be considered essential at any track facility. Most of the work of preparing the track area must be done at least a day before the meet, and an inadvertent rain will not erase permanent markings!

In checking the field events areas, the long jump takeoff board should be near enough to the pit to allow all jumpers to reach the landing surface. If it is not, and another board cannot be placed on the approach runway, lime or whitewash can be used to mark a temporary takeoff point. The sand in the pit should be spaded to make it a safe landing area. The high jump pit must be cleaned of any debris and the foam rubber landing pad must be arranged so that any high jumper, regardless of her skill, will land on the prepared surface. Areas where throwing events will be held should be roped off to prevent inadvertent encroachment which might be hazardous to non-participants. Often, for safety, these events are held in an area adjacent to but away from the track area.

Hurdles should be placed on the track early if such an event is to be the first race of the day. The judges' stand is placed in line with the finish line and about 20 feet from the track. The timers' stand should be set opposite that of the judges—a roped-off area in the stands will suffice. If no other space is available, the timers may stand in front of the judges. If at all possible, it is usually advantageous to have a common finish line, marked by white posts, for all races.

As much as possible should be done in regard to preparing facilities the week before the meet. Availability of equipment should be checked at least two months prior to the contest even though it might not be assembled in one place until a week before. The following is a basic check list for equipment:

*General*
    Chart of track showing places of events
    Bulletin board
    Number and safety pins for contestants
    Contestants' tickets
    Awards stand and/or table
    Rule book
    Scorer's table and chair
    Public address system (have another in reserve)
    Wet or dry lime marker for renewing lines
    Sharpened pencils
    Clip boards
    Officials' badges

*Track Events*

Properly adjusted stop watch for each timer
Whistles for starter and finish judge
Clipboards for clerk, chief timer, and chief finish judge
Cards (2″ x 3″) for each timer and finish judge
Yarn, soft white or orange, for the finish line
Day-glo arm band for the starter
Starter's pistol (.32 caliber with black powder blank cartridges)
Recall starter's pistol and blanks
Batons for relays
Hurdles (spares to allow for breakage)
Two anemometers (if records are to be authenticated)
Lane drawing bottle with pills (numbered cartridges may be used to draw
    for lane assignments)
Foul flags for relays

*Field Events*

Scale for weighing implements
Balance for checking javelin
Two crossbars for the high jump
High jump standards
Shot put and discus circles
Javelin (ball throw) arc
Beat board for standing long jump
Surveyor's pins for throwing events (each marked with a number)
Measuring tapes
    50 ft. for the running long jump
    12 ft. for the standing long jump
    12 ft. for the high jump
    50 ft. for the shot put
    200 ft. for the discus
    200 ft. for the javelin
    300 ft. for the softball throw
    200. ft for competitors to use to mark their long jump approach
Clipboards with instructions to chief judges
Score cards for throwing events ruled for preliminary and final recordings
Score cards for high jump ruled for three trials at each height
Foul flags for discus boundary lines
Rakes and brooms for long jump areas

## TEAM PACKETS

Packets should be given to the coach or a representative of each team as she arrives at the meet. Included in these kits should be heat and flight sheets, preassigned numbers with safety pins for contestants, time schedule, special instructions to participants and coaches, map of the track and field area, participants' tickets, tickets to social events, and meet programs.

## THE MEET

On the day of the contest, the director should plan to be at the track at least two hours before the meet is scheduled to begin. This should give ample time for a final check of equipment and facilities, and to greet early arrivals.

## SCRATCH MEETING

It is a good idea to have a scratch meeting—preferably the night before, but since many teams do not arrive until the day of the meet it may be necessary to schedule it an hour before the first scheduled event. The agenda will include change of entries in events, discussion of rules, and a question-and-answer period for the coaches. If it is not possible to conduct a scratch meeting, pertinent information should be placed in the team packet.

## POMP AND CIRCUMSTANCE

Glamour should be added to the meet in every way possible, but such effects must be kept secondary to the meet itself and should not add to the running time. An opening ceremony adds color and interest to an event involving numerous teams and participants. Usually this is of a patriotic nature involving a color guard, the raising of the flag, and, perhaps, music. A dignitary (such as the mayor, the host principal, or a representative of the sponsoring agency) may welcome the team and the contestants of the competing squads, or a team representative, may march around the track. The combined efforts of several groups—school and community service clubs, music, and ROTC departments—should be utilized whenever possible.

Color can also be injected through introduction of dignitaries and brief welcoming remarks by the home coach or the team captain. The provision of colorful and informative programs listing the schedule of events, comparative times, and pictures of performers always adds class. The queen idea is a relatively popular one, but perhaps a girls' track and field meet should have a king. The use of banners, flags, and music adds excitement, and they often are used.

## TIME SCHEDULE

A basic rule is to begin on time—if the meet is scheduled to begin at 9:00, *start the first event at that time.* The schedule given to the coaches and press prior to the meet should invariably be adhered to. It is a good idea to have a rainy-day schedule in reserve if the meet is an outdoor event.

## PRESENTATION OF AWARDS

Presenting awards with appropriate ceremony adds much to any meet, and gives the contestants special recognition. One of the most colorful procedures is to follow a ceremony with one such as that used in the Olympic Games. Awards may be presented by a businessman sponsoring the event, a well-known track personality, the president of the school board or PTA, a student leader, or any other dignitary. The public address system should be used in connection with such ceremonies to get spectators' attention. Such an announcement might be preceded by the fanfare of a trumpeter. If there is no special ceremony for awards, the usual procedure is for winners to simply pick up their prizes at the awards table. In this situation, standard practice is for the chief judge of each event to give place winners a ticket denoting their award, which is then presented by the athlete to the custodian of awards.

## POST-MEET CHORES

A social event for participants, officials, and coaches is a good way to end the day. Since many have a long distance to travel, the social may be limited to just a coke party to give everyone a chance to "warm down." Awards are sometimes presented at this time, and special recognition may be given to various individuals and groups who have contributed to the meet.

Results of each event (names, affiliations, and times or distances achieved) should be typed on a stencil as the meet progresses (see Fig. 41). Immediately following the final event, the information sheet should be mimeographed or xeroxed for distribution. Results should be called in or taken to all local and state news media—papers, radio, and television stations—as soon as possible.

The track area should be policed immediately for articles left by participants, officials, and spectators, and all equipment must be returned to the proper storage areas. The director should be especially careful to make sure that all borrowed equipment is returned immediately.

Thank-you notes should be written to all who helped, and the director should be lavish with her thanks and praise. If the meet is an annual event, the subsequent meet should be noted, asking for the addressee's assistance again. A letter should also be sent to the coaches of all participating teams and to the state high school activities association if the meet was sanctioned by such an agency. Information items should include the number of participants, numbers and names of schools represented, summary of events, team scores, individual records, and the date of the meet in the next season.

While everything is fresh on the director's mind she should jot down the names of the more effective officials, and pitfalls to be avoided in the future.

The final step of the director is to relax! If possible—even if for only a few days or a week or so—she should forget the just-concluded contest. All too soon advance planning for the next year's meet will have to begin, and a brief respite will aid in erasing the memory of the headaches inherent in a meet director's life. Putting on the show is fun, but even the most dedicated impresario needs a little time away from it all occasionally!

OKLAHOMA STATE MEET RESULTS
HIGH SCHOOL 19—

*Discus*
1. Sherrie Salyer, Stroud — 103'8''*
2. Mary Buchanan, Stroud — 90'9''
3. Susan LeForce, Jet-Nash — 88'3¾''
4. Lisa Steen, Putnam City — 84'7½''
5. Jackie Geis, Putnam City — 83'9¾''
 *(Old Record 100'6½'')

*Softball Throw*
1. Valarie Toombs, Enid — 183'
2. Kim Valviola, Putnam City — 178'7''
3. Alethea Lummus, Capitol Hill — 167'9''
4. Pat Bledsoe, Waurika — 167'6''
5. Jackie Geis, Putnam City — 166'

*High Jump*
1. Susan LeForce, Jet-Nash — 4'10''
2. Nan Oyler, Forgan — 4'9''
3. Karol Kvasnicka, Enid — 4'8''
4. Vanessa Thomas, Duncan — 4'8''
5. Theresa Hayes, Enid — 4'7''

*Standing Long Jump*
1. Rita Platt, Hennessey — 7'11¼''
2. Donita Metcalf, Jet-Nash — 7'8''
3. Margaret Dodds, Enid — 7'7½''
4. Debbie Chelf, Carrier — 7'7¼''
5. Casie Bond, Stroud — 7'6½''

*Running Long Jump*
1. Betty Peffer, Elk City — 17'2''
2. Mary Willingham, Stroud — 16'7''
3. Kim Hayes, Luther — 16'2''
4. Debbie Chelf, Carrier — 16'0''
5. Pat Bledsoe, Waurika — 15'11½''

*Shot Put*
1. Sherrie Sayler, Stroud — 38'3''*
2. Kaye McDaniel, John Marshall — 35'1''
3. Kirby Tate, Luther — 34'6½''
4. Roxie Bratcher, Jet-Nash — 33'3½''
5. Becky Perring, Enid — 31'10½''
 *(Old Record 36'3'')

*50 Yd. Low Hurdles*
1. Suzie Winningham, Hennessey — 6.9*
2. Sherri Salyer, Stroud — 7.4
3. Donita Metcalf, Jet-Nash — 7.8
4. Wendy Atkinson, Enid — 8.1
5. Kathy Savage, Rossevelt — 8.2
 *(Old Record 7.4)

*440 Yd. Run*
1. Dianne Eddiger, O.B.A. — 58.9*
2. Judy Sullivan, Union — 1:02
3. Linda Ward, Elk City — 1:03
4. Della McSpadden, Capitol Hill — 1:03.9
5. Nan Oyler, Forgan — 1:04.7
 *(Old Record 1:01)

*220 Yd. Dash*
1. Susie Winningham, Hennessey — 25.8*
2. Judy Sullivan, Union — 26.7
3. Rose Silver, Hennessey — 26.9
4. Janet Hickman, Duncan — 27.5
5. LaVerne Butler, Luther — 28.2
5. Dorothy Austin, Enid — 28.2
 *(Old Record 26.0)

*100 Yd. Dash*
1. Susie Winningham, Hennessey — 11.3
2. Judy Sullivan, Union — 11.5
3. Dee Ann Mahan, Yale — 11.6
4. Janet Hickman, Union — 11.8
5. Betty Peffer, Elk City — 11.8

*880 Yd. Run*
1. Rita Platt, Hennessey — 2:33.6*
2. Bene Sherfield, Luther — 2:34.6
3. Patty Kymes, Stroud — 2:37
4. Phyllis Frost, Hennessey — 2:38
5. Jeanette Mack, Waukomis — 2:46.1
 *(Old Record 2:40.5)

*440 Yd. Relay*
1. Hennessey — 52.0
2. Capitol Hill — 53.2
3. Waurika — 53.2
4. Luther — 53.8
5. Stroud — 54.1

*Team Score*
1. Hennessey — 37½
2. Stroud — 28½
3. Jet-Nash — 17
4. Enid — 15½
5. Luther — 12½

**Fig. 41.** Typical track meet initial results sheet.

# 14

# All Coaching Isn't Done
# on the Track

A girl performs well in her event at the track meet. After the race she exchanges congratulations with her opponents, dons her warm-ups, and walks to the victory stand to receive her accolade. She has the so-called look of the all-American girl with her happy smile, slender build, pony tail, and generally neat impression. The crowd applauds—the people appreciate her skill and her appearance. Several spectators may comment that she owes much of her success to her coach; however, few, if any, have any real concept of the time and effort that the coach has put into preparing this girl and her teammates for this day.

Months, possibly years, of planning go into producing the results that are shown by a girl at a meet and, hopefully, other results that are revealed by her in school, community, and family living. Each coach's plan will be different. The approach will depend upon her experience and philosophy. There is no one right way to coach just as there is no one correct way to run, jump, or throw. Whatever her methods, though, the coach must be sure that her objectives are established with the participants in mind. Their welfare is really all that matters. The coach's overall responsibility is to provide a program that will assist her girls in reaching their full potential in other aspects of their daily living as well as on the track.

## THE COACH

How is the success of a coach measured? By win-loss records, the actions of the girls on and off the track, the number participating in the programs, or the size and condition of the facilities she may have developed? What personal qualities of a coach contribute to her success however it is measured? These factors are very difficult to enumerate and name, especially in any order of importance.

148

The final test of the coach should not be the physical skill demonstrated by her athletes, but also the ways in which the team members respond to many other aspects of their daily living.  The typical coach has far-reaching influence on the total behavior of her girls, and her guidance can often contribute immeasurably, in *either* a positive or a negative manner, to the overall personality and well-being of each athlete.  Much of this influence will be concomitant with the teaching of motor skills during practice sessions, but other influences of the coach will be of a more indirect, and perhaps more powerful, nature.  The coach always presents a strong image, and because of this she is obligated to exhibit exemplary behavior in her own life.  Habits of language, dress, mannerisms, respect for self and others, honesty, promptness, and many other personality characteristics are transferable traits.  If a woman feels that maintaining such standards is an imposition on her personal freedom, she should seek work in which her influence on youngsters is less potent.

Not every coach can be highly skilled in the activity which she directs, but this is not an essential quality for success.  A much more important condition is that of caring enough to recognize the dual primary responsibility of looking to each girl's present and future off the track as well as to her performances on it.

Regardless of the size of the group, one works with individuals and no two girls are alike.  Of utmost importance is the need for two-way communication—the coach must be available to talk with her athletes and not just to them.  At the same time, the coach must remember her position—she is not their peer.  She should be fair and firm, neither criticizing nor praising too often without reason, and always she should talk in terms of success.  It is essential that the coach be technically well prepared and up-to-date on new ideas in skill techniques, training methods, and conditioning practices.

## SCHEDULE FOR THE YEAR

Practice and meet schedules should be ready to be given to the girls at the first meeting of the squad in the fall of the year.  Policies and procedures regarding the forthcoming track season should be discussed at this time.  These will probably be based on such factors as the philosophy of the coach, school regulations, skill level and motivation of the girls, events for which one is preparing, time of year, availability of facilities and equipment, climate, and budget.

### PRACTICE

Before any conditioning and training program begins, each girl should have a thorough medical examination, parental consent for her participation should be secured, and her eligibility checked.

The objective of the practice schedule is to prepare the girl for the competitive season. This involves training over an extended period of time, and for convenience this span may be divided into three parts—the off-season (September, October, and November), the pre-season (December, January, and February), and the competitive season (March, April, and May). Each daily practice session is normally divided into the warm-up, workout, and warm-down periods. The daily training schedule will vary for each individual and her specific event(s), and so there is no single, most desirable program of activities for all team members. Physiologically, however, the objective of the coach is to improve the efficiency of the cardiovascular system, increase the muscular strength, and develop improved joint mobility in each athlete. Most experienced coaches have accepted research evidence indicating that the following basic training procedures will improve these parameters:

1. Bursts of activity for a few seconds will contribute toward the development of muscle strength and longer tendons and ligaments.
2. Intense activity lasting for one minute, repeated after 4 or 5 minutes of rest or mild exercise, will contribute toward the development of anaerobic power.
3. Activity with large muscles involved at about 80% of maximum, lasting 3 to 5 minutes, repeated after mild exercise of similar duration, will contribute toward the development of aerobic power.
4. Activity at submaximal level lasting as long as 30 minutes or more will contribute toward the development of endurance.

Strength, flexibility, and endurance are developed most effectively over a period of several months—the first phase being devoted to general emphasis and the final effort to specialized emphasis. Whatever the program, it must be vigorous, continuous, and interesting.

## MEETS

Enough meets should be scheduled to make the season interesting and worthwhile. Nothing motivates hard work more than a good schedule. Meets should be set well in advance, preferably the year before. The team should be made aware of the committed dates, as this is only one of many schedules the girls will be following throughout the school year. Before preparing any schedule, however, the coach should confer with the appropriate school authority regarding pertinent policies. Factors to be taken into consideration include the budget, travel distances, students' time in regard to missing classes and study time, and the number of contests per week.

## RULES AND REGULATIONS

Training rules must be established and enforced on the basis of reason, with a logical explanation for each one. The participants must know what is expected of them before the program gets under way—everything pertaining to rules should be in writing and discussed at length at the first team gathering of the year.

### PRACTICE SESSIONS

Training rules and regulations vary with situations. A list such as the following should be provided for the team members:

1. Practice sessions will be held Monday-Friday from 3:30 to 4:45 at the track. If you will be late or unable to attend, inform the coach prior to the session. Otherwise you are expected to be in attendance.
2. Report all aches, pains, and other miseries to the coach. Prompt treatment may prevent additional troubles and your loss of training time.
3. Wear clean practice clothes. Soiled clothing not only indicates social carelessness, but also is a potential source of various types of infections.
4. Wear suitable and comfortable practice clothing—your training costume should match the activity you are engaging in and allow you to do what you are supposed to do. Unless the weather is quite warm, wear sweat clothes to aid in avoiding the ever-present threat of pulled muscles.
5. Wear canvas or rubber-soled shoes while warming up, and avoid unnecessary wear and tear on your legs by wearing spikes only when necessary.
6. Take care of your uniforms and equipment. Check out your own implements and return them to the equipment storage area each day.
7. Avoid wearing heavy make-up during practice. Hopefully, you will perspire, and the effect will be ruinous!
8. Dress your hair in such a manner that it does not hinder your performance or become a safety hazard.
9. Do not wear jewelry in practice or competition. Avoid the possibility of losing something of value and/or adding another safety hazard.
10. Follow your practice schedule. It was prescribed specifically for you—to protect you and improve your skill and physical condition. However, feel free to discuss any changes which seem important to you with the coach.
11. Shower after each session.

### INJURIES

First aid equipment and trained personnel to administer it should be available at all practices and meets. The coach should insist that participants report items such as blisters, athlete's foot, muscle pulls, contusions, abrasions, or any other injury or illness. The coach is not a doctor or nurse, but her training and background is usually such that she can take care of minor problems while referring those beyond her expertise to proper medical authorities. Generally speaking, treatment, other than first aid, by the coach should be avoided. Conceivably, it could be a dangerous practice in regard to the well-being of the girl, and, obviously, there are legal liability implications in such practice. Arrangements should be made with a local physician to serve as team doctor, and all injuries should be checked by him. Girls should not be permitted to practice or participate in a meet without a doctor's clearance, especially following a major illness or surgery.

## TRAVEL

Transportation must be planned according to school policy—mode (bus, private cars, school cars), drivers (other faculty, parents, regular bus driver), and insurance coverage. These plans should be formulated as the meet schedule is being made. Whatever the policies may be, they must be enforced—it is seldom a good idea to begin making exceptions to the rules.

Before each trip the itinerary should be given to parents. This should include information concerning where the team can be reached and what time to expect it to return. Travel dress should be simple and in good taste —styles and customs may vary but good taste does not. Travel dress for many teams is skirts and blazers, while others leave the choice to the girls. They may wear a dress, skirt and blouse, or a pants suit. Few teams, if any, wear such garb as jeans and sweatshirts for travel. Except in very unusual circumstances, grubby clothing is inappropriate when on the road.

Trips must be well planned. The team manager should be delegated the job of packing the equipment needed. The coach must know where the team is going and how to get there. Prior arrangements should be made with the home team in regard to dressing facilities. Expense money for meals and lodging, plus extra for emergencies, should be carried by the traveling coach. It is imperative that the team leave in time to allow arrival at the track a minimum of one hour before the first event is scheduled to begin.

If the trip is to be extended overnight, the planned schedule should provide time for any necessary practice, time for the girls themselves, time for meals, and time for rest. Free time to shop or visit a place of interest like the zoo or beach might be placed on the schedule. Regardless of the plans, time should not be allowed to hang heavy on the girls' hands, nor should they be permitted to loaf in the motel lobby or lounge.

In order for the girls to know what is expected of them, an information sheet such as the following may be given to them.

Please note the following comments concerning trips:

1. All trips are made for the primary purpose of participating in a meet. It is not a vacation trip. The team will travel together, stay together, and eat together unless special permission is secured from the coach.
2. On all trips you will be expected to make a well-dressed appearance. This means being neat and dressing in good taste—dresses, skirts and blouses, or pants suits may be worn, but jeans and sweat shirts or other overly casual costumes will not be worn.
3. The bus will leave at the scheduled time and return as near to the scheduled time as possible. Please note these times.
4. You are responsible for your own uniform and equipment.
5. Act, look, and speak in a ladylike manner. You are a representative of your school, and the impression you make reflects on many others. Smoking, drinking alcoholic beverages, cursing, using obscenities, and loud and boisterouus behavior will not be tolerated.
6. Be especially careful with your diet. Avoid fried foods, highly seasoned foods, extremely rich foods, and specific foods that do not agree with you. Eat as you would at home. **DO NOT OVEREAT.**
7. While en route to the meet, do not buy cold drinks, candy, crackers and such foods. This rule is relaxed during the return trip but it is not wise to cram your stomach with food at frequent intervals.
8. When ordering individual meals, observe the price limitations. Those ordering over the limit will be asked to pay for the difference.
9. You are assigned two to a room at the motel. Observe these room assignments and be in bed by 10:30 P.M. each night before a meet.
10. At the motel do not make phone calls, use valet service, order meals, or request other services from your room unless you pay for these at the time they are requested.

**EQUIPMENT**

Before the season begins, the coach must check the adequacy of first aid supplies, the condition of uniforms as to size and usability, and the availability and condition of facilities and equipment. Everything should be checked against an inventory list. This list should be kept up-to-date concerning the number of items on hand and their condition, when they were purchased and from whom, cost, and sizes. A specific storage area for each item should be established, and equipment and supplies should be kept in this assigned space. A check-out system that will accurately keep track of what is checked out, when, and to whom, should be provided. One person, perhaps the student manager, should be placed in charge of this operation. Each girl must be held directly responsible for any item checked out, including implements, meet uniforms, and practice uniforms. A pre-set return deadline should be adhered to. All items should be kept in excellent repair, and unsafe equipment should be disposed of.

## ELECTING A CAPTAIN

The selection of a student leader may be made before the season begins, after it gets underway, or at its conclusion, but it should always be the choice of the team. The selection should be made by secret ballot with no team member knowing the number of votes anyone received. The team's choice may not be the coach's choice, but the coach may utilize her judgment by appointing captains for different meets during the season, and then having the squad elect a permanent captain at the conclusion of the year. The coach's selections of meet captains may be based on the number of years in school, number of years on the squad, past performance records, or leadership qualities.

## BUDGET AND PURCHASING

A realistic budget for the next year should be prepared immediately following the season. This will be based upon the current year's expenses, the need for replenishing equipment and supplies, and any expansion to be made in the program. An itemized list to present to the school financial officer should be made including such items as equipment, facilities, uniforms, travel, lodging, meals, home meet expenses, phone calls, postage, medical expenses, awards, and repair.

If the coach is unsure of needs or costs, it is helpful for her to check with a more experienced coach or someone at least familiar with budgeting and purchasing. When purchasing, exactly what is needed should be described, and inferior substitutes should not be accepted. Orders should be placed early in the year—as soon as school procedures permit—and then only with reputable firms. Dealing with obscure business houses is a poor way to attempt to save money. All requisitions should be in writing and dated. If it is absolutely essential to order items by telephone, a confirming written order should *always* be processed immediately after such a purchase is made. Most requisitions and purchase order troubles stem from procedural deviations. Finally, request periodical financial statements from the school financial officer. Knowing how much money is in the budget and how that sum may be spent is not only good business practice but it also aids in avoiding financial troubles.

## MOTIVATION

A girl must be both capable and motivated before she can learn a skill and then perform at a level approaching her potential. The girl provides the capabilities, but the coach must provide the environment conducive to motivating her learning. Not all individuals are motivated by the same factors, so the coach will find it necessary to use different approaches to correspond with personality differences. Since such techniques are determined in part by an understanding of the girls involved, a coach must know the athletes with whom she is working.

In the school setting, the goals most often sought after by students are personal and socially oriented ones such as achievement, recognition, and belonging. If a coach can effectively contribute toward meeting these needs, she may be able to motivate the team members to achieve outstanding accomplishments.

Many different motivational techniques are used in coaching. The most obvious one, of course, is competition. This factor is an integral part of athletics, and the successful coach employs it as a primary tool. Not only is competition used in settings involving opponents, but a girl may be encouraged to compete against herself: to surpass her own best effort or the school record. Incidentally, competition is most effective when the athlete accepts the fact that there is a reasonable chance for the goal to be accomplished.

Another popular technique is the use of music. Little research has been done in this area, but it is logical to assume that certain types of music may result in increased excitability and thus to improved performance. Pep talks are often used and these may be logical and instructional, or tense and appealing to the emotions. The reward system works for some individuals. Reward may be in the form of praise, a school letter, travel opportunities, or a chance to make an all-star team. Other individuals respond more positively to punishment which may take the form of criticism, withholding of travel privileges, being denied the opportunity of posing for an action photo, or not being issued a uniform. Other techniques include giving knowledge of results (letting the girl know how good or how poor her performance was) or the showing of films of actual performance.

What motivates a girl at the beginning of the season may not serve the same purpose later in the year, and the coach must be alert to the need for changing the motivational environment. It should be remembered, also, that, strangely enough, some techniques that serve as motivators for one person may serve as reducers for another. Talks, films, reward, punishment, and music can be quieting as well as exciting.

## THE TEACHER-COACH CONCEPT

The conscientious coach is more than just a teacher of track and field skills. Because of the fact that she is the leader of an activity which the participants enjoy thoroughly and feel is important to them, she is usually looked up to, respected, and emulated by the girls. The coach is not only a teacher. Whether she wants to or not, at various times she serves roles as mother, big sister, counselor, close friend, and confessor. This is a heavy responsibility, but also a tremendous challenge and a continuing source of great personal satisfaction when the results of her efforts receive the nod of parental and public approval. Coaching is demanding of time and energy, it is often frustrating, and at times it is even heartbreaking. Invariably, though, there is the satisfying awareness to the coach that she is contributing significantly to the growth and development of the girls under her tutelage. All teachers do this, of course, but few classroom teachers have the variety of opportunities that the woman working with girls' sports has to influence her students for good or evil. This person, above all, must never forget: all coaching isn't done on the track!

# Selected References

BINFIELD, R. D. *The Story of the Olympic Games.* London: Oxford University Press, 1948.

BRESNAHAN, GEORGE T.; TUTTLE, W. W.; and CRETZMEYER, FRANCES X. *Track and Field Athletics.* 5th ed. St. Louis: The C. V. Mosby Company, 1960.

CROMWELL, DEAN B. *Championship Technique in Track and Field.* New York: Whittlesey House, 1941.

DAYTON, WILLIAM O. *Athletic Training and Conditioning.* New York: The Ronald Press Company, 1960.

DGWS *Track and Field Guide.* Current edition. Washington: American Association for Health, Physical Education, and Recreation.

DOHERTY, J. KENNETH. *Modern Track and Field.* 2nd ed. Englewood Cliffs, N. J.: Prentice-Hall, Inc., 1963.

———. *Modern Training for Running.* Englewood Cliffs, N. J.: Prentice-Hall, Inc., 1964.

DURANT, WILL. *The Life of Greece.* New York: Simon and Schuster, 1939.

FOREMAN, KEN, and HUSTED, VIRGINIA. *Track and Field Techniques for Girls and Women.* Dubuque, Iowa: Wm. C. Brown, 1971.

HENRY, BILL. *An Approved History of the Olympic Games.* New York: G. P. Putnam's Sons, Inc., 1948.

HOOKS, GENE. *Application of Weight Training to Athletics.* Englewood Cliffs, N. J.: Prentice-Hall, Inc., 1962.

JACKSON, NELL. *Track and Field for Girls and Women.* Minneapolis: Burgess Publishing Company, 1968.

KLAFS, CARL E., and ARNHEIM, DANIEL D. *Modern Principles of Athletic Training.* St. Louis: The C. V. Mosby Company, 1963.

*Official Track and Field Guide.* Current edition. New York: Amateur Athletic Union.

PALLETT, GEORGE. *Women's Athletics.* Dulwich: Normal Press, 1955.

PARKER, VIRGINIA, and KENNEDY, ROBERT. *Track and Field Activities for Girls and Women.* Philadelphia: W. B. Saunders, 1969.

PAUSANIAS. *Descriptions of Greece.* Trans. W. H. S. Jones and H. A. Ormerod. London: William Heinemann, Ltd., 1926.

POWELL, JOHN. *Track and Field Fundamentals for Teacher and Coach.* Champaign, Ill.: Stipes Publishing Company, 1971.

PUGH, D. L., and WATTS, D. C. V. *Athletics for Women.* London: Stanley Paul and Company, Ltd., 1962.

THORNDIKE, AUGUSTUS. *Athletic Injuries.* Philadelphia: Lea and Febiger, 1956.

WAKEFIELD, FRANCIS; HARKINS, DOROTHY; and COOPER, JOHN. *Track and Field Fundamentals for Girls and Women.* St. Louis: C. V. Mosby Company, 1966.

Magazines sources for track and field articles:

*Athletic Journal* (1719 Howard St., Evanston, Ill., 60202)
*Scholastic Coach* (50 W. 44th St., New York, N.Y. 10036)
*Women's Track and Field World* (P.O. Box 371, Claremont, Calif. 91711)